Please return or renew book
by last date shown above.

south
AYRSHIRE
C O U N C I L

Laid
Bare

Dick Kirby has also written:

Rough Justice – Memoirs of a Flying Squad Detective

The Real Sweeney

You're Nicked!

Villains

The Guv'nors: Ten of Scotland Yard's Greatest Detectives

The Sweeney: The First Sixty Years of Scotland Yard's
Crimebusting

Flying Squad 1919–1978

Scotland Yard's Ghost Squad: The Secret Weapon Against
Post-War Crime

The Brave Blue Line: 100 Years of Metropolitan Police Gallantry

Death on the Beat: Police Officers Killed in the Line of Duty

The Scourge of Soho: The Controversial Career of SAS
Hero Detective Sergeant Harry Challenor, MM

Whitechapel's Sherlock Holmes: The Casebook of Fred Wensley,
OBE, KPM Victorian Crimebuster

The Wrong Man: The Shooting of Steven Waldorf and
The Hunt for David Martin

Laid Bare

THE NUDE MURDERS AND THE HUNT FOR 'JACK THE STRIPPER'

DICK KIRBY

This book is dedicated to my chum, Bill Maclaurin.

His link with dubious company led to a flow of indispensable information.

And, of course, to Ann: till the stars grow cold

First published 2016

The History Press
The Mill, Brimscombe Port
Stroud, Gloucestershire, GL5 2QG
www.thehistorypress.co.uk

British Library Cataloguing in Publication Data.
A catalogue record for this book is available from the British Library.

ISBN 978 0 7509 6625 2

Typesetting and origination by The History Press
Printed in Great Britain

CONTENTS

ACKNOWLEDGEMENTS

F irst, I should like to pay tribute to my friend of twenty-plus years Alan Moss for his splendid foreword to this book; a fellow author and a former chief superintendent in the Metropolitan Police, Alan is a well-respected historian. I also wish to thank Mark Beynon, the Commissioning Editor of The History Press, for allowing him to bully me into writing this book. I'm glad he did; it has been a fascinating experience.

I wish to particularly thank John G.D. Grieve, CBE, QPM, BA (Hons), MPhil, Professor Emeritus; and Dr Peter Jerreat, MB, BS, B.Sc., DMJ (Path), Emeritus Home Office pathologist, for their very kind and thoughtful inputs to the book.

Next, Phillip Barnes-Warden, Metropolitan Police; Linda Bailey and Beverley Edwards, chairman of the Metropolitan Women Police Association; Bob Fenton, QGM, honorary secretary of the Ex-CID Officers' Association; Susi Rogol, editor of the London Police Pensioner Magazine; Barry Walsh, Friends of the Metropolitan Police Historical Collection; and Emily Burnell, senior pensions administrator, Equiniti Pension Solutions, all of whom were very helpful. Special thanks to my fellow author and friend, Stewart Evans, and his wife, Rosemarie, for their hospitality and assistance in researching this book.

There were a number of people I approached who, for reasons best known to themselves, refused to respond to my requests for information.

There were others who did so but asked me to respect their request not to be named and, of course, I have done so. And there were a small minority who provided pertinent assistance completely anonymously. Whoever you are, please accept my thanks.

Others who were not so shy appear in alphabetical order: Terry Babbidge, QPM; Brian Baister, QPM, MA; Robert Bartlett; Rod Bellis; Ken Bowerman, GM; Keith Buxton; Geoff Cameron; Janet Cheal; Bob Cook; John Cox; Roger Crowhurst; Mo Darroch; Kevin Gainford; Bob Hayday; Alan Jackaman; Bryan Martin; Jeannette McGeorge; Paul Millen; Michael Nadin; Michael Nesbitt; Barry Newman; John Newman; Gerry O'Donoghue; David Parkinson; Albert Patrick; the late Arthur Phillips; David Pritchard; Peter Quested; Leonard 'Nipper' Read, QPM; Bob Roach; Jane Rogers; John Strachan; Peter Westacott; David Woodland and Keith Yeulett.

Photos were supplied by Ken Bowerman GM, David Weir, David Woodland and from the author's own collection, and whilst every effort has been made to trace copyright holders, if there are any errors or omissions, The History Press will be glad to insert the appropriate acknowledgement in any subsequent printings or editions.

My thanks, as always, to my son-in-law, Steve Cowper, for guiding me through the minefield of cyber-land and my love and admiration goes to my children, Suzanne, Mark, Robert and Barbara, and to their children, Emma Cowper, B.Mus., Jessica Cowper, B.Mus., Harry Cowper and Samuel and Annie Grace Jerreat.

Most of all, my love to my wife Ann; together we escorted each other from the grip of that pernicious disease, cancer.

Dick Kirby, Suffolk, 2016

FOREWORD

The 'Nude Murders' that occurred near Duke's Meadows and the Heron Trading Estate in 1964–65 have all the hallmarks of the classic murder mysteries that have kept authors and journalists busy for many years, but they have never before received the authoritative analysis and style of attention given to them by this book. They were as serious as the Whitechapel Murders of 1888–89 by 'Jack the Ripper' and they shared many characteristics. They involved prostitutes and remained unsolved, despite many police resources being sent to the area. They engendered much speculation, by newspapers and others, about potential suspects, including well-known people or even a police officer. There were indirect connections to the concerns of the government, in this case the Profumo scandal. The Nude Murders have not generated books and TV programmes on the industrial scale given to the Whitechapel Murders, but that is not because they were any less noteworthy or intriguing.

Seventy-six years after the Whitechapel murders the police had the advantage of fingerprint technology and many forensic science techniques unknown to their Victorian counterparts, but the Nude Murders nevertheless remain unsolved. The perpetrator disposed of his victims' bodies in a far more calculating fashion than 'Jack the Ripper'. The investigation teams made heroic efforts, and spent countless hours and days searching for and cross-referencing information, necessarily using methods that today's computers would make redundant, if not laughable in some respects. Reputations were at stake in the Metropolitan Police. The world of prostitutes and their unsavoury clients is not something that is generally well known, even within most parts of the police, but the investigation made commendable efforts to work alongside this murky world of vice in order to catch the one crucial insight that might have led to the offender. Luck was not on the side of the police in this case.

Any police officer likes to know the inside story of who really did what, and many of us, especially when retired, like to air our insights into the mysteries that have covered the pages of the newspapers. Because the investigations are still within the living memory of some of the surviving officers from the team, this book, unusually, tells us what some of them thought about the case, and how they regarded the officers in charge of the investigation. We know some of the funny stories that occurred in those dark streets late at night. We can read about the enormous effort that was put in by teams of forensic scientists and how the mysterious marks on the victims' bodies were painstakingly traced to a specific location on a trading estate. We know the lines of enquiry that were followed, and can even consider the arguments about whether the cause of death was connected to the sex act that may have taken place. We know what the author thinks of people.

This book provides many valuable insights into a large-scale murder investigation and gives us an intriguing picture of the dark world of vice-related crime. This book gives us real history.

Alan Moss
www.historybytheyard.co.uk
Orpington, Kent
November 2015

PROLOGUE

Before this opus into the investigation of the murders of eight unfortunate young women gets under way, I need to advise you of a cautionary tale.

Nearly forty years ago, I was a detective sergeant in the Metropolitan Police and I was seconded to a murder squad in east London.

The circumstances were these: a 32-year-old housewife, who lived with her husband in a terraced house in a pleasant neighbourhood, appeared not to have an enemy in the world, with the exception of the person who had attacked her in the hallway of her home, as the victim answered the door to him – or her. She had been subjected to a ferocious attack with a sharp-bladed instrument that had left her lifeless body with so many stab wounds, front and back, that it was difficult to count them. It was, as someone remarked (and without the slightest hint at irony or disrespect) that she was 'as perforated as a postage stamp'.

And yet it appeared there was no motive for the attack – no sexual molestation, no robbery – and what was more, no weapon and no witnesses. Yet the hallway was splattered with the victim's blood in which the perpetrator would have been absolutely saturated and as he – or she – sauntered away, into the street in broad daylight, nobody saw a thing.

As most people know, the first twenty-four hours of a murder investigation are crucial; if clues aren't discovered then, they may never be found, so all of us worked hard to secure whatever evidence there was, as well as obtaining statements and making all the necessary enquiries. But as to who was responsible for this atrocious crime, nobody had the slightest idea.

It was late on that first night as the enquiry team finally sat down in the incident room; a bottle of Scotch was produced, uncorked and poured and comments were invited from the senior investigating officer, a detective superintendent. That was the norm then and, to my mind, a sensible tactic: a chance to wind down after the rigours of the day and to assess what had been done and discuss what needed to be achieved.

As suggestions were made, the superintendent nodded, murmured, 'Good', and to the office manager, 'Make a note of that.'

Suddenly, one of our number – and to save him any unnecessary further humiliation, I shall refer to him as 'John' – spoke up. 'Guv'nor,' he said. 'I've got a theory about this.'

'Yes, what is it, John?' asked the superintendent.

'The only thing is ….' replied John, hesitantly, 'Well, it is a bit outrageous.'

'John, as things stand, we've got fuck-all at the moment,' responded the superintendent testily, 'so if you got any ideas, let's have them.'

John smiled brightly and replied, 'Suicide!'

Never, before or since, in the space of thirty seconds had I heard so much concentrated, blasphemous, filthy abuse uttered by so many people focused upon one person. When the tirade finished there was a silence, followed by John, in a rather hurt voice remarking, 'Well, I did say it was a bit outrageous!'

'Let's book off duty, ladies and gents; early start tomorrow,' said the super-intendent briskly, giving John a piercing look that suggested that his days as a member of the murder squad might well be numbered.

Christmas came and went; still we were no closer to finding the person responsible. And then suddenly, a young woman put herself in the frame by making a number of comments that suggested that she might well be the guilty party.

Her name doesn't matter – although suffice it to say, I have never forgotten it, or her nickname – and she was an oddity. She had already tried to burn down a police station and was an obsessive pinball machine player, possessing enormous concentration to register high scores. She was not, she told me, a lesbian but she had a very masculine appearance, complete with cropped hair, a bulky physique and heavy boots and she was fanatical about boxing and martial arts. I spent hours on end talking to her about boxers, their fights and their training methods and she would come alive, joining animatedly in the conversation, adding comments of her own; but when I turned to the question of the murder, she shut up like a clam.

As I mentioned, there were no witnesses to the murder but there had been another murder committed a few miles away with a great many similarities to this one; and in that case, there was a witness – an off-duty bus conductor who had seen a suspect run off. He thought that this person was male – but that was exactly what my crop-haired, intrepid pugilist looked like. So I told her that I intended to put her up for identification in respect of that murder; she refused. I informed her that an identification parade was the fairest way of dealing with the matter and that the alternative was to be confronted with the witness. Still she refused, so I had the witness brought to the station and as she waited for the confrontation, she showed her first sign of emotion; she trembled uncontrollably, like a leaf in an autumn gale.

Now, I was in no doubt as to her culpability. The witness came into the room and looked at her for a full fifteen seconds. Finally, he turned to me and shook his head. 'I'm sorry,' he said. 'I just can't be sure.'

And so, I had to let her go. Eventually, with every avenue having been pursued exhaustively and fruitlessly, no arrests were made. The murder squad was wound up and I went on to pastures new.

But I never forgot the suspect. I had no doubt that not only was she the murderer in my case, she was also responsible for at least one other murder as well and I felt sick to my stomach that I'd had to let someone as dangerous as her out on the streets to possibly kill again.

While this did not become an obsession with me, even after two decades of retirement, from time to time, I still thought of her. And then one day, I bumped into an old friend who, coincidentally had carried out a 'cold case' review of the investigation. It transpired that my suspect was exonerated completely; the real murderer (now dead) had been identified beyond the shadow of a doubt. The other murder, for which she was put up for identification? It was not connected to the murder I'd investigated but it was linked to yet another murder, committed on the other side of London and that too was solved in a cold case review. Again, my suspect was guiltless; DNA on both victims matched that of the real perpetrator.

And therefore, the reason for this allegorical tale is this; as you read this book, don't have preconceived ideas, not like 'John' and not like me, either.

Although this book gets under way in 1959, there was a break until 1964 and then for more than eighteen months there was concentrated police work, the like of which had seldom been seen before. And when the investigations were finished, there was speculation, rumours and guesswork in the press, by writers and private individuals as to the identity of the murderer. Some were well founded, others fanciful and some unintentionally hilarious.

For the purposes of this book, you must become the senior investigator. You'll be in good company; some of the finest detectives at New Scotland Yard participated in these enquiries. Examine the facts and question everything. Look at the suspects; and my goodness, there's enough of them – twenty-six, in all. Is there proof there, or only suspicion? Those men from the Yard didn't think there was enough evidence but you might think differently. Were the various leads in the investigation pursued properly, or, given the resources available at the time would you, as the top detective, have taken a different course, have done things differently? As to that and in respect of everything else in this book, you must be the judge, with one word of advice from me. In the pages that follow, keep an open mind as to the identity of the murderer.

Professor David Canter, the eminent psychological profiler and author of many books, disagrees. In his excellent work, *Criminal Shadows*, he states, 'Senior investigating officers will say, "I have an open mind on this one", but no one can act with an open mind. There has to be some shape, some direction to make thought and action possible.'

I don't entirely agree. Yes, when a lead which appears promising emerges, then follow that line of enquiry and as that great detective, the Chief Constable of the CID, Frederick Porter Wensley, OBE, KPM, would tell his subordinates almost a century ago, 'Decide upon a line of enquiry and don't let anything or anybody deflect you from it until you are satisfied that you have gone through with it to the end.'

The point I'm making – and one with which I feel sure that Wensley and Canter would agree – is give that lead your best shot but when it's exhausted, unresolved, move on; don't be dogmatic but instead keep an open mind to other possibilities.

We'll start with an introduction to the world of prostitution and then, to paraphrase the late Bette Davis, 'Fasten your seatbelts.' What follows will be bumpy – no error there.

INTRODUCTION

should think that since time began, there have been prostitutes; for the
purposes of this book, whenever I use that term, I shall always be referring
to those of the female gender. Let me say (and without wishing to sound
overly moralistic), I have always thought that prostitution in the United
Kingdom should be legalised and that brothels should be government run.
In a clean environment, prostitutes would receive regular medical check-ups
to free them of unpleasant antisocial diseases, payment would be subjected
to income tax (a far less painful and a cheaper way than recompensing a
ponce) and the women would at least be comparatively safe from physical harm. Is that being excessively simplistic? I suppose it is. Right, moral
statement over.

So, prostitutes offer their bodies for the purposes of sex, regular or otherwise to men who, for an agreed sum of money, satiate their particular
wants – some kind of sexual gratification – while the prostitute satisfies
hers – money. Of course, things may change. With the rapid advance in the
realm of artificial intelligence, by the time this book is published, 'sexbots'
will be available for sale or hire. No argument there; these female robots
will be programmed to satisfy the most extraordinary demands of their
owners/leaseholders. I expect for an added thrill some of the sexbots will
be infected randomly with gonorrhoea with the excited punter not really
knowing if he might expect a dose of the clap. And think of the fun the

owner of a sexbot could have by knocking it about, without the threat of prosecution; slightly different for the renter of such an object, of course. The lessor of such a valuable piece of property would undoubtedly look askance at a bashed-up 'bot; after all, who'd want to hire an ugly android? Perhaps the renter would have to leave a sizeable deposit, returnable only when the owner had thoroughly checked the sexbot on return to ensure no damage had been inflicted, rather like the owner of a rented flat. Let's leave this technological world where anything might (and probably will) happen and concentrate on the better-known prostitutes, the living, breathing variety – although in the case of eight of them, not for too long.

Errol Flynn had dealings with quite a number of prostitutes worldwide (and also suffered from a number of deeply unpleasant sexually transmitted diseases as a result) but when he said, 'They may be sad, sick, victims, nymphomaniacs, or something else, but they deserve something better than any condemnatory term,' I agree with him.

Therefore, while prostitutes are referred to by a number of nicknames, most of them offensive, the one that I shall use from time to time throughout this book is probably the least disagreeable: 'toms', which was how they are inevitably referred to by the police. Their clients are known as 'punters' and the men who control the toms, to cater for their welfare, protect what they see as their investment, pay their fines and knock them about for whatever reason and whenever they think it necessary, are referred to as 'ponces'. Those who solicit for the prostitutes are known as 'pimps'. I should mention that in the criminal pecking order, ponces and pimps are in the lower echelons (the latter slightly more so than the former) and are looked down on by other criminals, the judiciary and the police. In fact, in the 1930s, one ponce who razor-slashed one of his flock and thought himself immune from prosecution was disabused of this notion when he was run to ground in a Covent Garden pub by that legendary detective, Jack Capstick, who was known to the underworld as Charley Artful. During his off-duty hours, Capstick played bowls and cultivated the beautiful roses that habitually adorned his buttonhole. On duty, his habits were not quite so benign. Capstick effected the ponce's arrest by drawing his truncheon and hitting him across the face with it, left and right, fracturing both his cheekbones, which also had the effect of wiping the smile off his face. He then completed the ponce's humiliation by dragging him all the way down to Bow Street police station through lines of cheering prostitutes. Bow Street police station is no more. Nor, unfortunately are cops like Capstick*.

Women convicted of prostitution were known, by virtue of the Vagrancy Act 1824, as 'common prostitutes' and this expression was used for almost 200 years until it was replaced with 'person'. Under the provisions of the Metropolitan Police Act, 1839, Section 54, sub-section 11 catered for the arrest of prostitutes who solicited to the annoyance of passers-by. The maximum fine was one of 40s (or £2) and that was the dire penalty imposed by the magistrates for in excess of the 100 years which followed. Since this niggardly amount could be replenished, back out on the streets in the twinkling of an eye, the toms in the dock could hardly wait to plead guilty. To dispute the charge meant all the longer spent at court, to delay going about their unlawful occupation, dismay their ponce and also to incur the displeasure of the arresting officer. Since the toms were pinched on a highly unofficial rota system, their usual moan was 'It ain't my turn!', although by upsetting the machinery of the courts by pleading not guilty, this was a sure-fire way of ensuring that 'their turn' came more regularly than was desirable.

By 1888, there were 5,678 prostitutes in London; however, this number related only to those who were known to police. In the Whitechapel area of east London their numbers were plentiful, due to the number of sailors returning to England after months at sea, bringing with them huge sums in wages of which they were only too glad to impart a percentage for a little sexual gratification. At that time, prostitutes were referred to in genteel Victorian circles as 'unfortunates'.

Emily Allen was referring to meeting her ponce, Morris Reubens, when she modestly told an Old Bailey jury, 'I was an unfortunate and he protected me against a man who was attacking me.' Unfortunately, this fulsome praise of her protector failed to save Mr Reubens from the gallows, since he was found guilty of murdering a sailor who was one of Miss Allen's clients.

The numbers of prostitutes in that area started to decrease at about that time, either by falling prey to the man who became known as 'Jack the Ripper' or by going on to pastures new, to avoid his depredations. But the

---

* For more about this famous detective, see *The Guv'nors*, Pen & Sword Books, 2010.

Whitechapel Murders were a stark reminder to those who made prostitution their precarious living of the dreadful risks that were allied to their occupation.

During the 1920s, fierce criticism of police by the judiciary and Parliament followed a number of high-profile arrests involving prostitution and although 2,291 arrests for that offence in London were made in 1922, the following year the number of arrests fell sharply to 650 due to the reluctance of police to take action through fear of censure, unjustified or not. In addition, a number of corruption scandals knocked the Metropolitan Police sideways and after the commissioner of police resigned, nobody else wanted the job. It was only when King George V intervened personally that his choice, Field Marshal Rt. Hon. Viscount Byng of Vimy, GCB, GCMG, MVO, reluctantly accepted the post – and made an excellent job of it.

However, new commissioner or not, prostitution was rife and by 1930 the commissioner had stopped inserting the number of convictions for prostitution in his annual report. But with the forthcoming coronation of King George VI in 1937, Mayfair residents complained about the number of prostitutes plying their trade in that area and demanded action from the police. They got it: and in that tiny section of London, policed by 'C' Division, 1,571 arrests were made. The following year, the number of prostitutes convicted in England and Wales stood at 3,192; of that number, again, the Metropolitan Police's 'C' Division covering London's West End, accounted for 2,298 of them.

The Second World War intervened and London was flooded with prostitutes to cater for the needs of servicemen on leave plus, of course, anybody else who required their services. A prostitute in the Mayfair area might earn as much as £100 per week (at a time when the average worker's weekly take-home pay was £5), although due to overhead expenses, i.e. her ponce, she would keep little enough of it. Many of the toms were orchestrated by the infamous Messina brothers, who enforced a rigid 'ten-minute rule' with their clients, although Gino Messina later 'increased production' so that on VE Day alone, one of his troupe serviced forty-nine servicemen. Several wartime prostitutes were revoltingly murdered by the psychotic Gordon Frederick Cummins; when he was caught, one of the toms fearfully asked the arresting officer, Detective Chief Inspector Ted Greeno if he was sure he had got the right man. When he replied that he was, and it was therefore conceded that it was safe for the West End prostitutes to resume plying their trade, Greeno was rebuked by the Assistant Commissioner (Crime) for encouraging them to solicit.

By 1955, the number of convictions for soliciting prostitution in England and Wales now stood at 11,878 – three years later, it rose to 16,700 – and it was clear something had to be done.

The Home Secretary, Sir David Patrick Maxwell Fyfe, GCVO, PC, QC set out a confidential cabinet memorandum in which he proposed heavier fines with imprisonment for repeat offenders in order to rid the streets of prostitutes, and this led to the forming of a committee of three women and twelve men, led by Lord John Frederick Wolfenden, CBE. *The Report of the Committee on Homosxual Offences and Prostitution* that was published on 4 September 1957 became known as The Wolfenden Report. Primarily, the committee dealt with legalising homosexual acts between consenting adults (which, in the 26 September 1997 edition of the *Pink Paper* led to Wolfenden coming forty-fifth in the top 500 of the lesbian and gay heroes list) but it also discussed street prostitution, which was regarded as a 'community instability' and 'a weakening of the family'. This led to the repeal of Section 54(11), Metropolitan Police Act, 1839 and placed The Street Offences Act, 1959 on the statute books. Now, a woman who had been officially cautioned twice for her behaviour by the police could be charged with being 'a common prostitute' and upon a first conviction be fined £10, and for a second conviction she could receive a fine of £25 or three months' imprisonment, or both. Additionally, the maximum sentence for living off the immoral earnings of prostitution was increased from two to seven years.

And it appeared to work. Practically overnight, the streets of Soho emptied, with hardly a prostitute in sight. From 16 August 1959 – the date on which the act was implemented – until 30 September 1963, 2,856 prostitutes were sent to prison, this number including 1,349 who were committed in default of payment of fines. That's not to say prostitution ground to a halt because, quite patently, it did not. Instead of enticing punters by soliciting them from the streets, printed cards were inserted in public telephone boxes that stated 'French maid offers services' and 'large chest needs polishing', complete with telephone numbers, and only the most dim-witted user of the telephone box could fail to understand their meaning. If the distributors of these cards were seen by police, that good old standby, Section 54, Metropolitan Police Act 1839 could be used. Although sub-section 11 had been repealed, sub-section 10 had not and it catered for the arrest of anyone 'who without the consent of the owner, shall affix any posting bill or other paper against … ' well, just about anything, really.

So, many prostitutes stayed in the Soho area, carrying on their trade in cheap hotel rooms or flats, where the hoteliers and landlords had 'no idea' of the names or occupations of their tenants. Others drifted away from central London where they undercut their Soho rivals by charging only a pound or two for their services.

Let me make one thing quite clear. The prostitute victims who feature in this book were not anything like the beautiful, exquisitely dressed 'Happy Hollywood Hookers' who featured in any of tinsel town's blockbuster movies and who entertained their equally glamorous clients in their pristine Beverly Hills apartments for hundreds or even perhaps thousands of dollars per liaison; neither did they resemble the jolly, 'tart with a heart' prostitutes as portrayed by Dora Bryan in several of the black and white, post-war British films.

The vast majority of these women had reached rock bottom; in a 1942 police report, these types of prostitutes had been rather disparagingly referred to as 'drabs'. Desperate for a few pounds, usually dependent on drugs, alcohol and a husband, boyfriend or ponce (and it was not uncommon for these three heroes to be melded into one), often riddled with venereal disease, sometimes pregnant, they hung about in dark, unfriendly places, sometimes accompanied by a ponce (but in the event of inclement weather, usually not), waiting for a punter to come along in his car to take them to an even darker, and possibly a far more dangerous, place.

One such area was situated near Chiswick and it was known as Duke's Meadows. Chiswick is a bustling area of west London, where just downstream from Chiswick Bridge, the crowds increase annually at the finishing post to witness the climax of the Oxford and Cambridge boat race.

A different type of climax used to be achieved in Duke's Meadows. In recent years the Duke's Meadows' Trust has undertaken extensive restoration work so that one of its latest attractions is a children's water play area, which opened in August 2006. However, this desirable state of affairs has only lately been achieved. Originally owned by the Duke of Devonshire, Duke's Meadows was purchased by the local council in 1920 to develop the area as a recreational centre, and in the years that followed, many of those who used its facilities put a generous interpretation on the term 'recreational'.

At the time of the murders, and for obvious reasons, it was known colloquially as Gobblers' Gulch and it was near there that the first body was found.

VICTIM NO. 1

ELIZABETH FIGG

Elizabeth Figg – she was also known as Anne Phillips – had never been convicted of any offence because her fingerprints were not on file at New Scotland Yard. Although there is absolutely no doubt that she was a prostitute, the courts had never punished her for soliciting prostitution nor had she ever been cautioned by the police for that offence. In fact, the very first time she came to the attention of the police was at 5.10 a.m. on 17 June 1959 when the crew of the night-duty area car, call sign Foxtrot Four, saw her lying with her back close to a willow tree. Behind her was Duke's Meadows and in front of her the River Thames made its brown, sluggish way down to the North Sea. Her eyes stared blankly at the river but she was unable to see it. She was quite dead and had been for several hours.

When the area car had patrolled this part of Chiswick previously – it was the Middlesex bank of the Thames and known as Riverside Lands – at 12.45 that morning, the body had not been there.

It would have been helpful if the area of Duke's Meadows had been policed adequately but it had not and this was due to a number of reasons. First, the commissioner of the Metropolitan Police (prior to the existing one, Sir Joseph Simpson, KBE), Sir John Reginald Hornby Nott-Bower, KCVO, KPM, OStJ must be held to account. He had a been a police officer all his life and a high-ranking member of the Met since 1933 but when he became commissioner in 1953 at the age of sixty-one, whatever get-up-

and-go he had possessed had got up and gone. By 1954, the crime figures at 93,937 were the best they had been since 1946, when they numbered 128,954; this, in no small part was due to the activities of the Ghost Squad. But that select team of detectives had unwisely been disbanded and now the crime figures surged. By 1958 they had reached 151,796 and the following year the number of indictable offences in the Metropolitan Police District had shot up to more than 160,000 – and that represented the worse crime figures of the century. However, the commissioner did nothing to curtail this alarming number of offences, nor did he do anything to support the pay and conditions of the police. Another 4,000 policemen were needed to supplement the existing 16,661 officers, but with conditions so poor and pay so low, nobody wanted to join the police and, in consequence, there were inadequate numbers of officers to patrol the capitol properly. Lastly (and quite apart from the crime figures) the police workforce was being stretched in a different direction. Public disorder was on the rise; it had commenced with the Notting Hill Race Riots of 1958 and officers had been hastily drafted in from all of the neighbouring divisions to deal with this civil disobedience, as they were with the CND's Aldermaston marches and the Committee of 100's protests. The government made it clear that they wanted this insurrection on the streets of London nipped smartly in the bud; the officers were overworked, exhausted and the overtime demands had stretched the Met's budget to breaking point. As the historian David Ascoli noted regarding the commissioner, 'He was a nice man when what was needed was a bit of a bastard.'

Therefore, those were the reasons why, on the night in question, the area of Duke's Meadows had only been visited twice by police in four-and-a-half hours – by car, not on foot.

PC Mills, the area car driver, made a quick inspection of the body. Figg was wearing a blue and white striped dress and an underskirt. The dress was torn open at the waist, which exposed her breasts, and there were scratches around her throat. The rest of her clothing, her brassiere, knickers and shoes, were all missing. So was her handbag.

Assistance was called for and Detective Chief Superintendent Ted Greeno MBE, the CID head of No. 1 District Headquarters, arrived. He had only three months to go before retirement with more than thirty-eight years' service but, being the detective in charge of the district, he wanted to view the scene first-hand. He was accompanied by his deputy, Detective Superintendent Leonard Woolner, plus Detective Superintendent James Mitchell, who would assume responsibility for the investigation.

Mitchell was a 6ft Scot from Alloa who had joined the police in 1931 following a five-year stint with the Royal Air Force. He was liked by his subordinates and referred to as 'Gentleman Jim', and he had served at the Detective Training School as well as two terms on the Fraud Squad. He was not really a murder investigator, he was a plodder. Of his thirteen commendations, nine were for his ability in cases of fraud.

However, that is not to decry his abilities as a detective; he got to work and the area between Barnes Bridge and Chiswick Bridge was sealed off and a shelter was erected around the body to await the arrival of the noted pathologist, Dr Robert Donald Teare, MA, MD, FRCP, FRCPath, LL.D, DMJ.

Following a cursory examination, the body was removed to Acton mortuary, where just over two hours after his initial inspection, Dr Teare carried out a post-mortem examination. At 5ft 5½in tall, Figg would be the tallest of the victims to come. There were a number of abrasions on her body, including several on the front of her throat. Several teeth were missing, it appeared that Figg had at some stage had a miscarriage, was suffering from venereal disease and there was dried blood at the rear of her anus which, said Dr Teare, 'could have been caused by a fingernail'. Figg had recently had sexual intercourse and Dr Teare believed she had died as a result of manual strangulation at about two o'clock that morning.

Three photographs were taken of the body at the scene, although it was claimed that, surprisingly, none were taken at the mortuary. However, one was. The corpse's eyes were propped open with matchsticks and the resultant photograph was published in the press. Meanwhile, an 'AS' (All Stations) message was sent out from Chiswick giving a description of the victim and asking the stations to search their missing persons registers. In addition, CID officers were drafted in from neighbouring stations on 'F' Division to assist in tracing witnesses and obtaining statements. On the opposite side of the river, the licensee of The Ship public house and his wife described how, on the night of the murder at just gone midnight, they had seen the lights of a car at the murder scene that were extinguished suddenly. There was the sound of a woman's piercing scream, which was extinguished as promptly as the car lights had been. This information was passed on to the murder squad and the usual systematic search of the area was carried out by the local uniform police, aided by the River Police, but nothing of any interest was found.

Within days, the photograph was recognised and Mrs Elsie King (who had remarried ten years previously) and her husband identified the corpse as that of her daughter, Elizabeth.

Born in Cheshire in 1938, Elizabeth Figg came from what used to be colloquially known as 'a broken home'. It was a dysfunctional family, which broke up, made up and rowed constantly. She drifted all over the country, starting relationships with men that often ended as soon as they started and commenced even shorter employments, in and out of London, until March 1959. It was about that time that she met Fenwick 'Baby' Ward, a native of Trinidad and Tobago. Also born in 1938, and weighing in at 15st, Ward had a fairly impressive record as a heavyweight boxer, having won ten of his fights, lost five and drawn one. It appeared that Figg was immediately enamoured with him, not least because, as she told her stepmother, 'he gets hundreds of pounds each time he wins a fight'.

However, it appears that Ward was being less than frank with her regarding his recent earning capacity because on 24 February that year he had appeared on the bill at Wembley Stadium and during his bout with Feleti Fred Kaho had suffered a technical knock-out in the first of what was intended to be eight rounds. It was Ward's first fight in fifteen months and also his last professional one.

Long before London became the welcoming multicultural city which, of course, it is now, several of Figg's friends, not noted for their high moral tone, looked askance at her new relationship. Ward arranged for her to move into a furnished room at Duncombe Road, Archway, N19, and it was then that she met a young East End prostitute, who moved in with her. Inelegantly referred to as Big Pauline, she was only 19 but she had already amassed a staggering thirty-three convictions for soliciting. Figg had commenced upon a short-lived life of prostitution only a few months prior to her death, soliciting with her new-found friend in the Harringay area at night and the area of Holland Park Avenue in the early hours of the morning. Ward apparently disliked their association, saying that they 'larked about' too much when he believed that Figg should be concentrating on earning at least £6 per night. Her clients were mainly men in cars and it was usually in their vehicles that sex, of whatever description, took place; neither Figg nor Pauline took their clients home.

Figg left Durley Road, N16, where she had been to see a seamstress, at about 9.30 on the evening of 16 June 1959 and said that she was going to catch a trolleybus to go to the Commercial Road. And she might have done; however, the fact remains that just over two hours later at 11.45 p.m. she met 34-year-old, self-employed builder Ernest Patrick Forrest at Endymion Road, N4. This was a mile from Durley Road and less than three-quarters of a mile from Duncombe Road. After having sexual intercourse in Forrest's car, he drove her to Holland Park Avenue, where she told him she had an appointment, and dropped her off at the junction with Lansdowne Road at 1.10 a.m. He made an appointment to see her again at 3.30 a.m. and drove around before returning to the area at 3.10 a.m. He was spoken to by two police officers at 3.20 a.m. and waited until 3.45 a.m. When Figg did not reappear, he went home.

If Forrest's account was right, then Figg could not have emitted the 'piercing scream' that was heard by the publican and his wife just after midnight, since she would have still been alive an hour later. Plus the crew of the wireless car had passed that area forty minutes later and the body was not there then. The pathologist's view that she had been murdered at about 2 a.m. would also therefore have been incorrect and consequently, whoever it was who had screamed, it could not have been Elizabeth Figg.

It is not known if she was alive or dead when she arrived at Riverside Walk but no effort was made to conceal her body and she was left at the spot either where she was murdered or dumped there shortly afterwards. However, it is certain that she arrived there by car. There was no evidence that the missing items of clothing were removed after death. Therefore, if that was the case, it appeared that all of her clothing and her shoes were removed prior to her death – either voluntarily or by her killer – and then following her death, she was partially re-dressed (this included her under-skirt) by the killer and her dress was torn open at the waist, if it had not been ripped open previously. It seemed a very odd business.

But twenty-four hours before Figg's murder, and less than a mile away from the scene, a 17-year-old girl was attacked by a man in Cromwell Road Extension, W4, as she walked home. He kicked her in the stomach, punched her in the face, tore at her blouse and tried to strangle her. As she collapsed on the pavement, he ran off. Could the two attacks be linked? Possibly.

'Baby' Ward told Figg's fellow prostitute not to tell the police that he had been poncing off her and made himself busy establishing alibis with friends at the time of Figg's disappearance, saying, 'a coloured man has got no chance in this country'. It was possibly one of the first times the race card was produced and since then, more than fifty years later, it has flourished. However, he need not have worried. Although Big Pauline did contact the police, during the two-month-long enquiry no real suspects surfaced.

On 18 June the inquest was opened and adjourned at Ealing Coroners' Court until 13 August, when the coroner, Dr Harold Broadbridge, heard evidence from Dr Teare, Superintendent Mitchell ('There was little doubt she was a prostitute,' he helpfully told the court) and Ernest Forrest – the last person to see Figg alive. The jury recorded a verdict of murder 'by a person or persons unknown'.

On 5 September, Figg was buried at Chiswick Cemetery. Only a detective and the undertakers were present; nobody else. It was a miserable end to an equally miserable life.

The typed statements were all collated and put into chronological order. Supt Mitchell prepared a report and the original statements, photographs and maps were attached to the rear of the file. It had been allocated reference 201/59/167, made its way to the Yard's repository for correspondence (it was known as General Registry) and there – for a bit - it stayed.

If Figg's murder was the first in a series of murders – and an open mind should be kept as to whether this was the case or not – then there was a long lapse of time before the perpetrator committed a further homicide. The reasons for this are many and obvious: imprisonment, confinement in a psychiatric hospital, travelling abroad plus, having killed once, fear of being caught. There is the possibility that the murderer died or committed suicide, but if that were the case, it would obviate the theory of a serial killer, at least one that included the murder of Elizabeth Figg.

But for the moment, Figg's murder was largely forgotten and time and crime moved on. In April 1960, 60,000 demonstrators protested vociferously against nuclear weapons and apart from making the police who attended the demonstration more fed up than before, it appeared to have little impact; six months later, Her Majesty The Queen went to Barrow-in-Furness, where to general acclamation she launched HMS *Dreadnought*, Britain's first nuclear submarine. Less than two weeks after that, Penguin Books was found not guilty of obscenity in the *Lady Chatterley's Lover* trial at the Old Bailey and as a result 300,000 copies of the book were printed immediately, of which 200,000 were sold in a single day. During the next eight months, sales would top 2 million – the permissive society had taken a large step forward.

The following year, on 8 March 1961, a young man named Edwin Bush was stopped in the street by PC Cole, who was an alert young copper. He had identified Bush as being the man wanted for the murder of an antiques dealer as the result of the first identikit picture being published; the identification was correct and Bush was hanged. Another identikit picture would feature in this enquiry, although not with the same amount of success.

A great deal of doubt was cast on correct identification a year later, on 4 April 1962, when a criminal named James Hanratty was hanged for the A6 murder. The controversy surrounding this case rumbled on for years and the investigating officer, Bob Acott DFC, was absolutely vilified. Like flies round a dung hill, the subsequent enquiries attracted the predictable left-wing brigade plus others desperate for publicity, and it was not until 2001 that, at the family's behest, Hanratty's body was exhumed. Alas, subsequent tests revealed beyond doubt that his DNA placed Hanratty well and truly at the scene of the murder; but it was too late for Acott, who had gone to his grave, his reputation utterly and unfairly tarnished. I wonder if Yoko Ono and her late husband, John Lennon, who jumped on the bandwagon and turned up at a London cinema seven years after Hanratty's execution waving a two-fingered victory sign in the air and sporting a ludicrous 'Britain Murdered Hanratty' poster, ever felt the need to apologise to Acott's family after Hanratty's guilt was established irrevocably? Just Ono, I mean; her husband had by then been murdered by a gunman who had fired double the amount of bullets than those used by Hanratty on his victim.

By 1963, civil insurrection showed no signs of abating; in April, 70,000 marchers arrived in London from Aldermaston to protest, once more, about nuclear weapons and, once more, police arrived in large numbers to be knocked about and generally abused in the name of 'peace'.

However, in August, the world of crime was turned upside down when approximately fifteen determined men stopped the Glasgow to London mail train in Buckinghamshire and helped themselves to £2,631,684. Weighing 1½ tons, the booty vanished – and so did the culprits. The public was agog at such an audacious crime and there were mixed emotions about it; one bowler-hatted toff who was filmed in the City of London, drawled, 'Jolly good luck to them,' and it was not thought that he was referring to the police. Within weeks of the robbery, the Flying Squad executed 419 search warrants and the press was buzzing with everything and anything to do with the Great Train Robbery.

So when a prostitute named Gwynneth Rees got into what might have been a Ford Zephyr Zodiac on 29 September 1963, it was not of the slightest interest to anyone, except that it was casually noticed by a fellow prostitute. And when her body was discovered six weeks later, it did prompt headlines in the *Daily Mirror*: 'Girl dead in pit – murder probe starts' – but not for long; world events would overtake any interest that might be generated in that case.

More than four years had lapsed since the murder of Elizabeth Figg. The question was: had the same man killed Gwynneth Rees – and if he had, was he the same person who would murder six more prostitutes in the fifteen months that followed?

VICTIM NO. 2

GWYNNETH REES

Few prostitutes have a happy, stable start in life and Gwynneth Rees was no exception. Born in Barry, Glamorgan, in 1941, she ran away from home aged 16 after her mother died. Rees was a pretty, dark haired, brown eyed girl, who commenced a long series of often meaningless relationships with men and in 1958 she gave birth to a baby girl. She stayed with her sister (who brought up the child as her own) in Canvey Island, Essex, but was obliged to leave after her sister objected to her bringing a variety of men back to her home. Rees travelled to London and used the streets of Whitechapel as her regular beat to solicit prostitution – she also used the alias Tina Smart.

In 1959 Rees was stopped by police for soliciting in Stepney and a year later she was pregnant again, this time the child was aborted. In January 1962, she met 20-year-old Micky Calvey and they lived together. In May, Rees was sentenced to one month's imprisonment for soliciting. Following her release, she lived with prostitutes in Poplar and Stepney, and in November 1962, she was released from prison, having served a three-month sentence – in all, she would notch-up thirteen convictions, mainly for soliciting – and, again, she was pregnant. The father was Calvey, but following her son's birth, the couple were separated once more after Calvey was arrested and later sentenced to a term of imprisonment.

While Calvey was on remand, Rees was accosted by a gang, the leader waving a chopper in a threatening manner, and although it is not entirely clear why, this could have been because she should have been endeavouring to raise funds for Calvey's defence – and it was suggested the ringleader was his friend, George Dixon. However, this was later strenuously denied by him.

In March 1963, Rees was pregnant once more and living with a convicted ponce. A month later, she met the very violent Cornelius Whitehead, who also ponced off her. ('That's news to me!' exclaimed 'Nipper' Read when I mentioned it to him, more than fifty years after the event, but at that time in the 1960s Read had not commenced his enquiries into the brothers Kray and Whitehead would not feature in Read's investigations for another five years.)

In June, Rees was admitted to hospital after haggling a price with a punter who drove off in his car. Since her handbag was inside the car and she was unwilling to relinquish ownership of it, she was dragged along, attempting to retrieve it. The following month, she was found to be suffering from venereal disease.

Getting disenchanted with Whitehead and his incessant beatings, she moved in with Victor Hatt, a twice-convicted ponce. However, her nemesis, in the form of Whitehead and his associate Michael Holland, caught up with her and they meted out a thrashing that left her black and blue.

Her final conviction for soliciting was in August 1963, when she was conditionally discharged at Thames Magistrates' Court; her last known address was Hague Street Buildings, Bethnal Green.

Rees was last seen wearing a full-length brown and grey imitation leopard-skin coat with a wide collar on 29 September 1963, getting quite willingly into a Ford, which might have been a Zephyr, close to the junction with Commercial Road and New Road.

Nothing more was heard or seen of her until two o'clock on the afternoon of 8 November 1963 when Patrick Cyril Dineen, the driver of a Richmond and Barnes Council digger truck, was loading a lorry with clinker from the refuse tip at Townmead Road, Mortlake, on the south side of the Thames, less than a mile away from Duke's Meadow. Buried 2ft under the rubbish was the badly decomposed body of Gwynneth Rees. Due to the actions of the digger, the corpse was badly damaged: teeth were missing and the head had separated from the body, which was naked save for one 15 denier nylon stocking that had originally cost 4s 11d per pair and which had rolled down to her ankle.

Detective Chief Superintendent John (Jack) Mannings from No. 1 District Headquarters and Det. Supt Frederick Henry Chadburn from 'V' Division arrived and took charge of the investigation. Prof. Arthur Mant MRCS, LRCP, MBBS (London), MD, MRCPath, FRCPath, MRCP, FRCP also arrived, wrapped the body in plastic sheeting and had it conveyed to Kingston mortuary. An eminent pathologist, Prof. Mant would succeed Dr Keith Simpson as head of the department of pathology at Guy's Hospital Medical School after Simpson's resignation in 1972.

The following day, police started sifting through tons of rubbish at the site looking for a murder weapon plus any other clues and, at the same time, Prof. Mant carried out a post-mortem examination. He was able to say the body was that of a woman, possibly aged between 20 and 25, 5ft 3in in height, who had probably died between one and two months previously. Most of the intestines had putrefied and much of the body was in an advanced stage of decomposition. Who she was and how she died was a mystery.

However, the police at the scene had found three of the corpse's eight missing teeth and also the hyoid bone. This horseshoe-shaped bone – it is also known as the tongue bone – is situated between the chin and the thyroid cartilage, embedded horizontally in the root of the tongue. In practically every case of manual strangulation, the hyoid is broken and in this instance the right-hand horn was missing. It was thought that the hyoid had been fractured at the time of death or shortly afterwards and that the cause of death was strangulation; but the fact remained there was a possibility the fracture could have been caused by the digger. A second stocking that matched the one left clinging to the corpse's ankle was also discovered at the site, but apart from that there was no trace of Rees' coat with the wide collar, nor any other of her clothing or possessions whatsoever.

And there were few clues to go on, either – no photograph, no clothing. Nevertheless, the usual investigations were carried out and with an incident room set up at Richmond police station. The description (such as it was)

was circulated with the request for enquiries to be carried out of surrounding stations' missing persons registers, and at local boarding and guest houses and hotels for women who had failed mysteriously to return. In those days, each station kept a Special Enquiry Register, which contained details of all those establishments, plus pubs and clubs, as well as many other useful addresses, so it was straightforward for constables patrolling their beats to ask their questions and report back. The Special Enquiry Registers have long since been consigned to the dustbin, as have beats and constables to patrol them.

It was just possible to extract a small amount of skin from one of the corpse's fingertips. A search at the Yard's fingerprint department was made but it was not until 26 November that it was revealed that it belonged to Gwynneth Rees – alias Tina Smart of course, but also known as Tina Wales, Tina Rees, Georgette Rees and Tina Dawson. Like many prostitutes, Rees was a stranger to the truth.

However, by then world events had rather overtaken the publicity surrounding the murder investigation. Four days previously, the American president, John F. Kennedy, had been assassinated in Dallas, Texas, and two days after that his killer (this, I know is still controversial) Lee Harvey Oswald was murdered, right in front of the television cameras, by Jack Ruby. In between those dates, and on the home front, the first *Doctor Who* programme was broadcast and three days after the discovery of Rees' identity, *I Want to Hold your Hand* was released by the Beatles to the general acclamation of many pre- and post-pubescent girls on both sides of the Pond.

It appeared that the death of Gwynneth Rees was considered pretty small beer by comparison, since the press now had far more interesting matters for their readers. These included the sensational arrest of train robber Roy James, who leapt 30ft from the roof of a flat in St John's Wood into the arms of the Flying Squad. However, now that Rees had been identified, Fred Chadburn and Jack Mannings, both experienced investigators, plunged straight into the enquiry.

Chadburn then had thirty years' service and as the Company Fraud Squad had opened its doors for the first time in 1946, he had been one of the first to enter and won commendations for his investigations into cases of fraud, false pretences and fraudulent conversion. But he had also been praised for his work in cases of infanticide and murder and he was in good company with Jack Mannings who, with barely two years' service in 1933, had been commended by the commissioner and awarded £2 after he arrested two suspects who threatened him with a revolver and assaulted him. Spending four and a half years' service with the post-war Flying Squad, as well as carrying out arrests for the Ghost Squad, Mannings knew his way around the seedier parts of London. With his involvement in the investigation of the Jack Spot/Billy Hill gang wars of the 1950s, this included its inhabitants.

They discovered that most of Rees' life as a prostitute had been spent in east London, but not all of it; she had also solicited in the West End, Battersea and, according to *The Times*, was 'well-known in the Angel area of Islington'. Owing to the variety of names she had used, this made it extremely difficult for investigating officers from west London, for whom the East End and the surrounding area was practically a closed shop. The police were regarded as the enemy in this part of the capital, where talking to the law was discouraged and grassing to them was tantamount to a death sentence.

However, the investigators were not discouraged and with the aid of the local officers, they steamed right into the middle of the East End's criminality. People on both sides of the law did speak to them with Whitehead the first of eight people to be pulled in, and he was held for two days. He initially denied that Rees had ever been in the back of his Zephyr Zodiac, then admitted she had and acknowledged beating up Rees. When blood of the same basic grouping as Rees' was found on his clothing, the back seat of his Zephyr Zodiac and also his father's car, a Ford Classic that he sometimes used, he confessed it might have come from Rees during one of his four admitted attacks on her. He denied poncing off Rees, any more than he had admitted poncing off three other prostitutes whom he had – allegedly – attacked. Holland, too, was brought in – he had a conviction for causing grievous bodily harm with intent – and he too admitted assaulting Rees, but both of them denied killing her. However, witnesses were forthcoming who would say that Whitehead had threatened to push Rees in the Thames and immerse another prostitute in a canal.

George Dixon was also questioned. He denied waving the chopper or threatening or assaulting Rees in any way, saying he knew and liked her. He had also known and liked Ronnie Kray, although their relationship became somewhat soured after an altercation in the Green Dragon Club in Aldgate, when Kray had pulled a gun on him. It misfired and Kray gave him the cartridge, telling Dixon to keep it as a souvenir. He did. When Rees had told a witness she was terrified of going anywhere near the Kray ancestral home in Vallance Road, Bethnal Green, the gallant Kray twins were brought into the melting pot. Shielded by their solicitor, Mr Sampson, they refused to answer questions or even look at a photograph of Rees. This is not to suggest they were in any way culpable regarding Rees' murder; their aversion to meeting the police with or without legal representation stemmed from the fact that at that time they were earning £100,000 per year from their long-firm frauds alone, quite apart from their income from racketeering, plus casually slashing and/or shooting anyone who displeased them. It was a two-way street; the police loathed them, which was demonstrated when Reggie was charged with housebreaking and then Ronnie and brother Charlie were charged with being 'suspected persons, loitering with intent to commit a felony'. Both cases were chucked out at court after the witnesses (both for the prosecution and the defence) had been 'straightened'.

Messrs Mannings and Chadburn had done a thorough job; not only were all the suspects thoroughly interrogated, their clothing and their cars (where they possessed them) were searched scrupulously for forensic evidence and their alibis tested and re-tested, all to no avail. There was insufficient evidence to charge anybody with Rees' murder.

At the inquest held at Kingston Coroners' Court on 4 March 1964, before Dr Cyril Baron and a jury, Brenda Meah, the prostitute with whom Rees had lived in Poplar and was the last independent witness to see her alive, told the jury that if indeed it had been a Zephyr Zodiac into which Rees had stepped, it was *definitely* not the one that belonged to Cornelius Whitehead. The court was also told by several witnesses that at the time of her disappearance, Rees was pregnant and that she intended to either self-abort or find a backstreet abortionist. This did have the ring of authenticity about it; Rees knew a number of people who had been (or were about to be) convicted at the Old Bailey for procuring abortions. More than 1,100 witnesses had been interviewed by police and Prof. Mant believed she might well have been strangled and that her clothing had been removed after death. But the cause of death could not be strictly ascertained and therefore the jury had little alternative but to return an open verdict. One week later, she was buried at St Katherine's Church, Canvey Island.

So why did Gwynneth Rees die? There is little doubt she was deeply involved, in one way or another, with the East End gangster scene. Did she discover matters for which it was decidedly unhealthy for her to know – or did she speak out of turn, perhaps once too often? Did she, perhaps, acquire the services of an illegal abortionist who botched the job, stripped off her clothing to avoid identification and buried the body? Or did she fall prey to a depraved serial killer, whose first victim's body was discovered some four years' earlier on the opposite side of the Thames, less than a mile away?

★★★

On 5 March 1969, Reginald and Ronald Kray were each sentenced to life imprisonment for murder (not, it should be emphasised, the murder of Rees), with a recommendation from the judge that they serve at least thirty years. Cornelius Whitehead (who was then serving a two-year sentence for possessing forged American dollars) was sentenced to seven years, to run consecutively, for being an accessory after the fact to one of the Kray's murders. Whitehead had previously been acquitted with George Dixon for causing grievous bodily harm with intent to a club owner, but on 4 July 1972, Dixon was one of a gang convicted of involvement in protection rackets and generally causing people quite serious bodily harm. He was sentenced to twelve years' imprisonment.

Micky Calvey, father of Rees' son – who might possibly have been able to bring something like normality into her life – was shot dead by police in 1978 while carrying out a robbery. Shrieking, 'Murderer!' to the officer responsible, Calvey's widow, Linda, went on to serve three years for robbery and later became enamoured with Ronnie Cook, who was serving sixteen years, also for robbery. When Cook was due for release, Calvey offered £10,000 to a Danny Reece to murder him. Reece wounded him, whereupon Calvey, according to the prosecution, took the shotgun herself, shouted 'Kneel!' and shot and fatally wounded her paramour. In 1991, both were convicted of murder (with Ms Calvey volubly proclaiming her innocence) and sentenced to life imprisonment. She and Reece were married in prison but later separated. Released in 2009, Ms Calvey married George

Ceasar, a retired businessman, who was seventeen years her senior – like Linda, he had been married twice before – and it was hoped that the couple would live happily ever after.

Alas, it was not to be. After five years of marriage, 84-year-old George passed away during the weekend of 5 September 2015 in a Spanish hospital from natural causes. Although he had allegedly told his friends, 'Marrying Linda was the worst mistake of my life,' and she had supposedly told her friends that, 'she wasn't prepared to sit around at home in God's waiting room, day in and day out,' Linda, who it was said had rejected proposals of marriage from such luminaries as Reggie Kray and 'Mad Frankie' Fraser, was said to be concerned at nonsensical rumours that she had married Ceasar for his money. Living in Basildon, Essex, and – because of the amount of time she had spent behind bars – said to be living on a state pension of just 11 pence a week, one can only hope that in the very near future, Linda Ceasar née Calvey, formerly Reece, Prison No. TT0377, finds long and enduring happiness.

It was very much symptomatic of an average episode of the popular television series *EastEnders* (who probably glean their material from unhappy little scenarios such as this).

And for those pundits who slavishly praise books written by (or on behalf of) East End gangsters from the 1960s, sagely observing, 'Well, wimmen could walk the streets in safety in them days', this homily did not extend to Gwynneth Rees, who was unfortunate, both in the Victorian, as well as the present day, sense.

VICTIM NO. 3

HANNAH TAILFORD

Two prostitutes dead, both discovered on opposite sides of the River Thames. Both of them were naked with the certainty that one of them had been asphyxiated and that the other probably had. Almost four-and-a-half years had separated their deaths. Was there a link between them? It was a possibility, nothing more. But in less than three months after the discovery of Gwynneth Rees' body, another corpse of a woman was found. She, too had been a prostitute, she too was naked, and she was not near to the Thames, she was in it.

This was the thirty-first homicide of the 296 committed in the United Kingdom during 1964. During the years that followed the Second World War, the number of murders carried out in London would remain reasonably stable; with the coming suspension of the death penalty, the figures would rocket.

The body was discovered at 1.15 p.m. on Sunday, 2 February 1964 by two brothers, Douglas and George Capon, who were preparing for a boat race on the Thames that afternoon. Both were members of the Corinthian Sailing Club and the body of the woman, naked except for nylons around her ankles, was now on the Hammersmith foreshore, her head jammed beneath a pontoon.

The police were called, an incident room was set up at Shepherd's Bush police station and the investigation was taken up by DCI Ben Brynmor

Devonald of C1 Department (usually, but erroneously referred to as The Murder Squad), New Scotland Yard. His police service, which commenced in 1936, had been interrupted by war service as a colour sergeant major with the Special Investigation Branch of the Military Police but since his demobilisation he had climbed the ranks, making a name for himself as a hard-working copper. He had spent nearly four years with the Flying Squad and it was now that he was reacquainted with the man who had been christened Rueben George Frank Ridge (but who was always known as 'Frank'). Ridge had spent more than six years with the Flying Squad and, like Devonald, he had been showered with commendations. Now, since 1960, Ridge had been a detective inspector attached to 'TA' Division – otherwise, the River Police – and it was in this capacity that he assisted the chief inspector.

At 215 miles, the Thames is the longest river in the United Kingdom. Starting at Thames Mead, Gloucestershire, it passes through forty-five locks and flows under in excess of 200 bridges before reaching the North Sea via the Thames Estuary. The River Police, which had been formed in 1798, patrolled the Thames to prevent river-based crime and to promote safety on the water. At its height, 216 officers manned thirty-three motorboats from seven stations, covering the 51 miles from Erith to Shepperton. On average, the police recover sixty dead bodies from the river each year. Others are saved and nowadays this is mainly due to the fact that the Thames has really cleaned up its act; more than 120 different species of fish populate the Thames, including Bottlenose dolphins as well as seals and hundreds of thousands of birds. But not at the time of this incident. In 1957, the Thames had been declared 'biologically dead' and anyone who entered those murky waters voluntarily for any reason was extremely unwise.

The body was taken to Hammersmith mortuary where, later that day, a post-mortem examination was carried out by the pathologist Donald Teare. The body, which was covered in mud, was 5ft 2in tall, with brown hair and eyes. There were surgical scars on the abdomen, teeth were missing and those that remained were nicotine stained and filled extensively. The woman's nails had been bitten voraciously and there was bruising on the lower jaw that had been caused prior to her death. These bruises could have been consistent with blows from a fist, although it was impossible to say how long before death they had occurred. The contents of her stomach revealed an undigested meal and the lungs had 'ballooned' with water from the Thames therein, with froth and fluid in the air passages, all of which were consistent with drowning. What was not was the fact the woman's semen-stained knickers were stuffed inside her mouth.

Hannah Tailford – identified by her sister and her fingerprints (although Tailford was also known as Theresa Bell, Anne, Hannah and Mary Lynch and Anne Taylor) – had been born thirty years earlier in Northumberland. By any stretch of the imagination, her moral and criminal behaviour was appalling. From the age of 15 she was clearly beyond the control of her parents; promiscuous and convicted of larceny, she was sent to an approved school and there she remained for three years. Within three months of her release she was again convicted of larceny and was placed on probation for two years with a condition of residence, and within six months she escaped. Arrested for breaching the probation order, the magistrates, perhaps unwisely, ordered that the probation order should continue, again with an order of residence, and again she absconded. Committed to borstal training, she escaped, was recaptured, returned, released and recalled, and then once again, interspersed with convictions for soliciting prostitution, she was returned, released and recalled to borstal training.

Tailford had taken up with 24-year-old William Ewing (who called himself Allan Lynch) in 1956 and they lived as man and wife. Aged 25, Tailford was pregnant; this matter was disposed of by placing an advertisement in a newsagent's window at the end of April 1959 offering the baby for sale when it arrived to 'a good home'. By doing so, she had contravened Section 50 of the Adoption Act 1958, which had been placed on the statute books eighteen days previously and which provided both for the giver and the receiver of persons of exchanging a child for money to a fine of £400 or three months' imprisonment. Not that this fazed Tailford, who was now calling herself Mrs Theresa Foster, any more than it did when a reporter from the *Sunday Pictorial* arrived at her hovel at Filmer Road, Fulham. Telling a piteous story of being deserted by her merchant seaman husband, she declared that her actions were 'wicked and shameful' but what else could she do? Her husband was on the seven seas, she had no money and her parents were both dead. Her son was born on 5 June – the father was, of course, Lynch – and she duly handed the child over to a Staffordshire couple in return for £20. Neither the giver nor the receivers of the baby boy were prosecuted.

There were more court appearances for larceny from an employer and when – allegedly – she found a chequebook and a driving licence in a paper bag in the gutter and forged a cheque, she was sentenced to a total of three months' imprisonment. During the following two years, two more children, a boy and a girl, were born with the boy being adopted immediately. Tailford and Lynch were now living in Battersea and the little girl was looked after by a local woman when Tailford went out to solicit prostitution. The couple moved from one dreary address to another, often through eviction, leaving a mountain of debts and unpaid bills and with Tailford lying outrageously to anyone who would listen about her supposedly deceased children and the man (not Lynch) whom she was going to marry. She had a vicious temper and an alcohol problem, as well as taking amphetamines, which were then known as 'purple hearts'. It was said she attended 'kinky parties' or 'orgies' at Dolphin Square that had been arranged by one of the occupants, a foreign diplomat named André. He told her he was French but was a little economical with the truth. His name, sounding very much like André was, in fact, Andrei and he was on the staff of the embassy of the Czech Republic. When former DI David Woodland went to interview him, no trace of him could be found, either at Dolphin Square or at the embassy's premises at Kensington Palace Gardens. 'My only thought at the time was that his immediate superiors may have felt he could be vulnerable to an approach by our security services and, as a precaution, he was returned home,' Woodland told me, adding reasonably, 'This, of course, was pure speculation on my part but there was a certain amount of logicality to this!'*

Tailford was also involved in pornographic photography sessions, which involved the inclusion of lesbians, vibrators and – perhaps – unsuspecting customers. This led to the question: was she involved in taking compromising photographs of her clients and then blackmailing them? At the time of her disappearance her large, black patent leather handbag had contained a

---

* For further adventures of this intrepid officer, see *Crime and Corruption at the Yard*, Pen & Sword Books, 2015.

purse that was known to have contained £27 18s 0d, plus a rather full diary that might have held details of her clients. But those items, together with much of her clothing – a flame-coloured nylon blouse, a black cardigan and skirt and black leather court shoes, together with a wristwatch and gold wedding ring – were never found.

She had previously met Thomas Trice, a rather strange, retired bachelor who was used really as a 'gofer', someone handy to decorate the flat, shift furniture around and also to accompany her on shopping trips (which he often paid for) while he was heavily made up, dressed in women's clothing and was known as Auntie Gwen.

In January 1964, the Lynch family moved into a top floor flat at Thurlby Road in West Norwood and on Friday 24 January she left at 9 p.m. – according to Lynch he did not see her alive again. Also according to Lynch, during their eight-year relationship, he was convinced that Tailford was employed as a cashier in an all-night restaurant in Southwark Bridge Road. Right.

A witness who knew Tailford from a café in Victoria saw her walking along Endymion Road on 29 January, and eighteen people supposedly saw her on various dates between 24 January and 1 February. And then in the early hours of 1 February, the downstairs neighbours at Thurlby Road heard the sounds of footsteps on the stairs up to the flat, music being played and then the sounds of a woman screaming.

Lynch's friends, who had been present that evening, were interviewed – as was Lynch – but denied there had been a woman present. Later the same day, Lynch had given 'Auntie Gwen' clothing and a pair of shoes belonging to Tailford, telling him to 'get rid of them'.

When the *Daily Mirror's* headlines of 5 February proclaimed 'River Nude: Man helps Yard' they were referring to Allan Lynch, who the previous evening had wandered into Lavender Hill police station in what was described as 'a highly distressed state'. Following Lynch's interview by police, the clothing and shoes were recovered from 'Auntie Gwen's' home in Kent. The shoes had mud splatters on them, but apparently the amount was insufficient to detect a comparison either on the body or with the mud on the banks of the Thames, where the body had been found. The investigation threw up a lot of red herrings. Tailford was enamoured with a man named 'Del' whom, she said, she was going to marry. This would have presented problems for the RAF corporal in question, since he already had a lawfully wedded wife and four children; it did not preclude him from being interviewed, at length. The cashing of a stolen cheque sent detectives racing to Southend but as far as this investigation was concerned, it led nowhere, as did the discovery of a police warrant card and a driving licence, the property of a serving officer, which had allegedly been in Tailford's possession.

'I was on the first and the last of the Nude Murders, the only murder squad employing more officers at the end than it had at the beginning,' former DC John Newman told me. 'Officers on the first murder squad were employed daytime checking on addresses supplied by prostitutes of clients who were violent, or liked to manually strangle whilst having sex and/or the use of stimulants. Hannah Tailford was an out-and-out prostitute who would do anything for anyone,' he continued, and added that while making enquiries in the cafés in which Tailford had previously visited, he was also subjected to Cilla Black, whose 1964 hit, *Anyone Who Had a Heart* was constantly blaring out of the jukeboxes.

According to an up to date (and ill-informed) source, 'Given the fact that the victim was a prostitute, the police naturally weren't that concerned about investigating the matter'. This absurdly pompous statement fails to explain why, during the three-month long investigation with lamentably poor resources, the police were able to question more than 700 people, or why the areas of Duke's Meadows and Barnes Common were searched systematically, why the River Police used creep drags to search the bed of the River Thames or why enquiries were made at houseboats from Chelsea to Chiswick, as well as the investigations that were made at hotels and lodging houses. The concept that police were unconcerned regarding the scope of the investigation simply because Tailford was a prostitute is fatuous.

And on 19 February, the same day as the actor and comedian Peter Sellers and the Swedish starlet Britt Ekland commenced an ill-fated marriage, River Police discovered a woman's blue coat that had fouled their boat's propeller; it was not only identified as belonging to Tailford (which had been given to her by 'Auntie Gwen') but at the inquest, held at Hammersmith Coroners' Court on 28 April, it was positively identified by a witness as the coat Tailford had been wearing when he had last seen her on 31 January.

The same witness stated that at the same time she was depressed and had spoken of taking her own life, and additionally she was, 'as high as a kite' on purple hearts (although no traces of amphetamines or alcohol were found in her stomach). Lynch told the inquest that, on the day of her disappearance, Tailford had asked her little girl, 'How would you like a new mummy?' It is possible, of course, that Tailford was either joking or perhaps contemplating discharging her responsibilities as a parent, as she had with regards to both her sons. Lynch – who disclaimed paternity for Tailford's two sons – also told the inquest she had given birth to a child before they met; it may or may not have been true.

Devonald – thanks to the assistance and expertise of the River Police under Ridge's command – had deduced that with regard to the tides and currents of the Thames, it was likely that Tailford had entered the water in the vicinity of Duke's Meadows. He told the inquest of Tailford's lamentable lifestyle, including the fact that apart from her convictions for dishonesty, she also had three convictions for soliciting prostitution. He also mentioned that during some of her sexual encounters she was prone to strip naked.

Donald Teare gave his opinion that the body had been in the Thames between two to seven days and, referring to the bruises on the jaw, suggested they could have been caused either by a blow from a fist or a fall. Regarding the semen-covered panties found stuffed in Tailford's mouth, Teare said he had heard of instances where suicides had stuffed items in their mouths to prevent their screams from being heard. However, suicides do not normally enjoy a full meal before stripping naked (apart from the nylons rolled around her ankles) and, even though the temperature at that period was outstandingly mild, at 12.3°C, immersing themselves in the River Thames. The coroner, Dr Gavin Thurston, told the jury that suicide was 'wildly improbable' but nevertheless, they returned an open verdict.

And so Hannah Tailford was laid to rest. Just over a year later, Ben Devonald also died of a heart attack aged 50 while still serving as a police officer. The lives of two people on the opposite sides of the fence that governs law and order were extinguished, rather more prematurely than they might have been.

Devonald left behind a wife and three children; like Tailford, two boys and a girl. Unlike Devonald, Tailford, however, left behind a lot of unanswered questions.

VICTIM NO. 4

IRENE LOCKWOOD

Nothing of real importance had happened during the first fifty-four years of Kenneth Archibald's life. He had never been convicted of any offence, his attempt at a childless marriage had failed after five years and a year later, in 1947, he left the army and joined the Merchant Navy. Between then and his death in 1972 aged 62 there were just three items of significance in his otherwise humdrum life and they all happened on 27 April 1964.

First, he reported to police a break-in at the premises where he worked; he may, or may not have organised or been implicated in the crime. Later that day, he appeared at Marlborough Street Magistrates' Court, where he was remanded on bail in respect of an entirely unconnected charge of larceny. This related to the alleged theft of a hearing aid; his own one was being repaired and when he was loaned another, he kept it. Although he pleaded guilty, the magistrate refused to accept his plea – it was probably qualified with the remark, 'I took it but I didn't mean to keep it' – and therefore it was possible that he was innocent of the charge. And finally, he walked into Notting Hill police station and confessed to murdering a prostitute; and of that offence, he was most certainly innocent. All this arose from the discovery of a corpse, almost three weeks earlier … .

★★★

The body of Irene Charlotte Lockwood was found at Corney Reach on the Thames foreshore on the morning of 8 April 1964 by a member of the River Police. There were certain similarities with the case of Elizabeth Figg, who died some five years earlier, as well as Hannah Tailford, two months earlier. All were prostitutes, all were naked with teeth missing and all had been found within a few hundred yards of each other, all on the north foreshore of the Thames; Lockwood's body between the other two. All that, plus semen was found on both Tailford and Lockwood's vaginal and oral swabs.

The officer informed the head of the River Police's CID, DI Ridge, and then searched the area of the foreshore. It would later be discovered that Lockwood was last seen wearing a check-patterned coat, a black skirt and what were described in the fashion of the day, as 'kinky boots', but he found no trace of these items, nor, indeed anything else of any relevance. Lockwood was aged 26, about 5ft tall with blonde hair and between her shoulder and right breast was a wound, measuring 6½in long. This had been caused after death so it is possible that a boat's propeller had been responsible. During the post-mortem that was carried out by Donald Teare he discovered that Lockwood had been between fourteen and eighteen weeks pregnant with a baby girl. There was no evidence of sexual molestation, she was unconscious when she entered the Thames, there was water in the lungs that had 'ballooned' and in the absence of any pre-death injuries the cause of death was given as drowning. It was thought that she had been immersed for no more than forty-eight hours. Interestingly, her body was described as 'dirty' but the matter was taken no further than that. It is possible that whatever the nature of the grime, it was of a type more likely to adhere to her body; if it was common or garden dust or dirt, certainly immersion in the river for a day or two would have washed it off. This matter is mentioned purely because of what was found on the bodies of the victims yet to come.

So was it all as simple as a straightforward case of misadventure? Frank Ridge obviously thought not. He informed Det. Supt Frank 'Jeepers' Davies at Shepherd's Bush police station and Ben Devonald (who was still investigating the Tailford murder) moved over and made more room for a fresh enquiry. Davies had served two terms with the Flying Squad and had been commended by the commissioner on ten occasions, so he was well-known to the other two officers – in fact, he would go on to head the Flying Squad and be appointed MBE.

A tenacious detective, Davies was aged 48 and at just 5ft 9in, with a prematurely balding head and a small moustache as befitted a former wartime army lieutenant, he now set about working backwards; to discover who the murdered girl was, what she had done, where she had been, who she had associated with and who saw her last – and who had killed her? He certainly believed that someone had indeed killed her, 'mainly' (as was noted in *The Times*), 'because of the mystery of the missing clothing' and because she had been immersed for such a short amount of time it was considered impossible that the tides and currents would have dragged away her clothes.

The first part was easy: fingerprints and a tattoo, 'John in Memory' (this possibly being the father of her child), revealed her identity together with a shabby and interesting lifestyle. Lockwood was illegitimate and left her native Nottingham at the age of 19 to travel to London, but not before she had acquired her first conviction in 1956; it would be the first of fourteen diverse offences – mainly soliciting.

She had given birth to a child in 1958; a boy who was placed in care. She broke up with the child's father, formed another relationship until that too dissolved, and was reunited with her former partner until a prison sentence for him brought about another separation.

Davies and his deputy, DI Dick Chitty, who the previous year had helped investigate the Great Train Robbery, dug deeper into Lockwood's life.

A year before her death, Lockwood had worked with another prostitute, Vicky Pender – she was also known as Veronica Walsh – posing for indecent photographs and blackmailing the clients thereafter; Pender was found murdered at a flat in Islington on 19 March 1963. Suspicion fell upon Colin Welt Fisher, a former paratrooper and the possessor of some 500 indecent images of the women, but he stated that at the time of the murder he had been staying at a hotel with a girl named Sandra Lockwood. 'Sandra' was one of the aliases Lockwood used with her surname; 'Barbara' was another, as well as Sandra Russell and Barbara Norton.

But whatever name she was using, Lockwood wisely denied being with Fisher at the material time, which was just as well, because he was later found guilty of Pender's murder and sentenced to life imprisonment.

Since that time, she had worked as a hostess at a number of dissolute West End clubs and lived at Flat No. 2, 16 Denbigh Road, London, W11; to assist with the exorbitant rent of £12 10s 0d per week, another prostitute moved in with her.

Lockwood ran quite a lucrative business; bringing a punter back to the flat, both would undress and whilst they were both busily engaged in the bedroom, Lockwood's ponce would help himself to the contents of the punter's wallet. She was not averse to having sex in the punter's car and was also amenable to anal sex. The last time she was seen at the flat at Denbigh Road was at 10 p.m. on Friday 3 April when there was a blazing row with a man who was heard to say, 'Don't be stupid!' She left shortly thereafter, owing two weeks rent.

At the time of her disappearance – she was last seen alive at 8 p.m. on 7 April at the Windmill public house, Chiswick High Road, when she was wearing the same check coat as shown in her photograph – she was pregnant, once more; the father's identity was debatable.

On 10 April an inquest into Lockwood's death was opened at Ealing Coroners' Court. Her landlady, Pamela Edwards, provided identification of the body (but only after the coroner, Dr Harold Broadbridge had permitted her to write down her name and address), saying, 'I identify the body of the woman I know as a Mrs Sandra Russell. She was not related to me' – and with that, the inquest was adjourned until 8 May.

★★★

Kenneth Archibald was employed as an odd-job man at the Holland Park Lawn Tennis Club, Addison Road, West Kensington, with free accommodation in a basement flat. He received a modest weekly wage of £1 10s 0d, which supplemented his service pensions, making a total of £5 16s 7d. The resident caretaker, Joe Cannon, organised illegal drinks parties after the club had officially closed, which attracted a motley collection of punters, prostitutes, night-club hostesses and – Irene Lockwood.

On the day following the discovery of Lockwood's body, DC David Bretton (who twenty years later would become the detective chief superintendent at King's Cross police station) interviewed Archibald. The reason for this was because a card had been found in the handbag in Lockwood's flat with a telephone number – PARK 7157 – that corresponded to the call box outside his flat, with 'Kenny' written on the reverse. This was sufficient to tie him in with the telephone number, but Archibald was also shown a photograph of Lockwood and denied having ever seen her before; however, this was quite untrue.

And now, nearly three weeks later, on 27 April, Archibald had reported a break-in to police, had appeared at court and had been remanded on bail. In addition, he started drinking at The Colville pub in Notting Hill. He was getting more and more anxious, and his companions suggested that it was due to the court hearing regarding the hearing aid theft. However, Archibald told them, 'It is more serious than that. You do not know how serious it is,' and when he suddenly declared, 'I'm going to the nick,' he did just that.

'Initially, he asked for me, because I'd had previous dealings with him,' former DC Barry Newman told me, 'but I wasn't there, so he spoke to DC Stan Moorehead.' This was the officer to whom Archibald had earlier reported the break-in and he told him that he wanted to give himself up. Understandably, Moorehead thought that he was referring to the break-in (which would have confirmed his suspicions about Archibald) but was also justifiably shocked when Archibald replied, 'No, I pushed the girl in the river; you know, the blonde, Lockwood, at Chiswick.'

'You did *what*?'

'I killed that girl Lockwood. You know, the girl whose photograph you showed me when you came to the club.'

He was asked, 'Are you sure?' which elicited the reply, 'I am sure.'

Taken to Shepherd's Bush police station, Archibald was interviewed by Supt Davies, who asked him, 'Are you saying you killed the girl?'

'Yes, I was drinking. I killed her,' replied Archibald. 'I have got to tell someone about it.'

He then volunteered the following written statement:

I want to tell you the truth because it has been on my mind. I had been drinking in a number of public houses and shortly before closing time I went into the saloon bar of the Windmill pub in Chiswick High Street. I saw the girl standing at the bar. She was a blond. I got into conversation with her and bought her a gin and tonic.

She asked if I fancied going for a short time with her. I said, 'Yes'. We left the pub and arrived at the river sometime about 11pm. There were no people about and she asked for £4 and said she wanted some money first. She insisted on having the money first. I must have lost my temper because I had my hand around her throat. She did not scream. She did not make a sound.

She fell to the ground. I decided to take her clothes off. I am not sure why I did this. It may have been that if she was found in her clothes people in the pub might have been able to connect her with me. I then proceeded to take her clothes off and roll her into the river. I took her clothes, bundled her clothes up and walked home. I put them on the living room fire, and the following afternoon took out the ashes and put them in the dustbin.

Now, it is common for some people, for any number of reasons, to go to a police station and falsely confess to serious crimes. Generally, they possess mental health issues and by the time they have finished their confession, it is clear from the number of inconsistencies they have put forward that they cannot possibly have been responsible. And had that been the case with Archibald, he would probably have been impolitely but silently categorised as 'a nutter', courteously thanked for his time, told that the matter would be investigated carefully and sent on his way.

Certainly, there were discrepancies. The murders of Lockwood and Tailford had already been linked. Therefore, had he also murdered Tailford? He had not. He stated that he had not had sexual intercourse with Lockwood (and if true, this was just as well since she was infected with gonorrhoea) and although semen was present in her mouth and vagina, it was possible that this was the result of an encounter with one or more punters.

However, the licensee of the Windmill recalled that Lockwood *had* been in the pub that evening, although he could not recall seeing anyone with her. Therefore, that partly corroborated Archibald's confession. Donald Teare was shown Archibald's statement and, although he stated that he would have expected to have found abrasions on her body, there was nothing in the statement that was inconsistent with his findings. There was the business card with the tennis club telephone number on it, with

'Kenny' on the reverse. In addition, a diary was found in which the same telephone number was also written and for the week commencing Sunday 5 April, in the same writing, were the words, 'Kenny is coming April 2 or 3 Thursday. He is young and handsome'. (With regards to this entry, it is felt that Lockwood was either referring to another 'Kenny', or if she was referring to Archibald, that she had exceptionally poor eyesight or a rather outrageous sense of humour.) A woman told of how she found a carrier bag containing women's clothing in Archibald's wardrobe, together with a photograph that 'she was sure' was of Lockwood; unfortunately, before she could give evidence her mental state had degenerated to such a degree that she was admitted to a psychiatric hospital. A witness was found who told of Archibald's 'temper tantrums', a divisional surgeon (a police doctor) decided that the prisoner was sane, once again Archibald repeated his confession, took the detectives to where he and Lockwood had allegedly met and where he had apparently carried out the killing and he was duly charged with the murder of Irene Lockwood.

So it appeared that there was a sufficient amount of evidence to charge Archibald. However, the night before his first appearance in court there was a hastily convened conference at the Yard and it was called by Deputy Commander Ernest George William Millen CBE, known (behind his back) as 'Hooter', either because of his imperious nose or the fact that, disdaining internal telephones, he roared his demands down the Scotland Yard corridors. Davies and Millen had known each other on the Flying Squad in the 1950s when the former was a detective inspector and the latter, a detective chief inspector. During that time, Davies had been commended for his actions in cases of armed robbery and for arresting 'a persistent criminal'. However, there were a number of 'Spanish Practices' that abounded at that time, including the use of 'mugs' – dupes used by criminals to shoulder the blame for thefts of lorry loads for which they themselves were responsible – and participating informants where a gang of robbers would be arrested just prior to the offence being committed, leaving one of the members of the team to escape despite there being sufficient numbers of officers present to quell the most aggressive Notting Hill carnival. Millen was determined to bring a halt to this type of behaviour and when he took charge of the Flying Squad in June 1961, he stated, 'It is the 1960s and this has got to stop.'

Not that Davies was thought to be part of any kind of questionable behaviour but when he arrived at the Yard on 30 April he was questioned closely as to the strength of the evidence surrounding Archibald and was told, quite unequivocally in Millen's irresistible style, 'Make sure you've got the right fucking bloke!'

However, Davies was in a cleft stick. 'The Director of Public Prosecutions had said to Jeepers, "Can you find evidence to prove that he *didn't* do it? If not, charge him",' Barry Newman told me.

The evidence was tested at Acton Magistrates' Court, where Oliver Nugent, on behalf of the Director of Public Prosecutions, outlined the facts of the case, in which he referred to Archibald's 'rather eventful day'. Nugent told the magistrate, Major Charles Fisher, 'The case against him rests simply on a series of confessions he made to police three weeks after the body was found,' and on 22 May 1964 the magistrate decided that there was a sufficiency of evidence to commit Archibald for trial.

Two months passed, with Archibald in custody before he appeared at the Old Bailey on 19 June 1964 and before Mr Justice Nield pleaded not guilty. During the five-day trial, E.J.P. Cussen led for the crown, the witnesses gave their evidence and Archibald stammered that he had only made the highly incriminating statement because he was depressed and confused. After fifty-five minutes' deliberation, the jury accepted his explanation and Archibald tottered from the court, a free man.

As Major Cussen, the prosecuting counsel, had not had a lot of success. During the Second World War, as a member of MI5, he had investigated the author P.G. Wodehouse, who had made a series of humorous broadcasts to the United States while interned in enemy-occupied Europe at the behest of the German government. Although Cussen exonerated Wodehouse of any treasonable activity, the author (who referred to Cussen as being 'a priceless ass') never returned to England; Wodehouse, who had written more than ninety books, is still one of the most popular and prolific writers in the English language – and ironically and coincidentally, Kenneth Archibald was a devoted fan. Cussen, whose fortunes improved after the collapsed trial of Archibald, went on to become a high court judge.

So was this a perverse decision by the jury? No, it wasn't. Had Archibald, in fact, murdered Lockwood? No, he hadn't. But not only had he confessed, he had absolutely insisted that he had murdered her; there was evidence to support his confession and that being the case, Davies was obliged to charge him. The case had been aired at the lower court and the magistrate decided there was enough evidence to commit him for trial. So, why did he confess? Was it 'the desire to be great' that was mentioned as one of a human being's most important aspirations in Dale Carnegie's 1936 best-selling book, *How to Win Friends and Influence People*? Quite possibly. Was it his need for 'fifteen minutes' worth of fame' in a life so empty, so humdrum that it almost defied comprehension? Again, quite possibly because, even after his acquittal, he was still embellishing his accomplishments, telling the press that he, rather than Joe Cannon, had opened the drinking club and hinting roguishly at 'a gay lifestyle', although this, of course, was prior to that term being used as an acronym for homosexuality.

'He was a complete fantasist,' Barry Newman told me and since Archibald had written him a series of cheery letters while on remand in prison, Newman was subpoenaed by the defence, although seeing the way matters had progressed during the trial, he was never called to give evidence about the remarkable letters.

The inquest at Ealing Coroner's Court on 8 May 1964 returned a verdict of 'drowning' in the absence of any other evidence, including one important point. Unlike all the other victims, Irene Lockwood's body showed no sign of clothing marks after death. In all the other cases, the underwear marks, by the blanching of the skin, were most obvious.

So Kenneth Archibald, short, dumpy and deaf (who, with some justification, could have been nicknamed 'Norman No-mates') wandered off, to spend his remaining eight years in anonymity. It was not thought necessary to interview him about Helene Barthelemy. Three days before Archibald had made his impassioned confession, her body was discovered. She, too was a prostitute; and despite the verdict at the Coroners' Court in respect of Lockwood, she too had been murdered.

Not, however, by Kenneth Archibald. 'Bill Marchant never believed Archibald's story and neither did I,' Barry Newman told me, adding, 'I always thought the murderer was a copper.'

VICTIM NO. 5

HELENE BARTHELEMY

I t is quite possible that police did not immediately connect the deaths of Figg and Rees with this sudden spate of murders but following the demise of Tailford and Lockwood, the discovery of a third prostitute's naked body in under three months (together with all the speculative comments in the press) spurred the hierarchy at the Yard into action.

The most senior officer to arrive at Barthelemy's murder scene was the man in charge of the CID at the Yard, Commander George Horace Hatherill, CBE. Towering over his subordinates at 6ft 6in, chain-smoking Hatherill spoke six languages, had served in both World Wars and had been a member of the Metropolitan Police since 1919. In 1933, his linguistic skills were not found wanting when he went to Poland to help smash up an international counterfeiting gang, and as a detective chief inspector in 1941, Hatherill had successfully solved the murder of two little girls who had been stabbed repeatedly by a soldier. He had been helped, in no small part, by a 12-year-old boy named Norman Page, who was a brilliant witness and who stood up to the most searching cross-examination in court. After the case, telling Master Page that he was 'a clever boy', Hatherill suggested, 'When you grow up, you ought to be a detective,' and received the crushing reply, 'What, me? Sit on my arse doing nothing all day? Not bloody likely!'

Accompanying Hatherill, and almost as imposing, was the deputy commander, Ernie Millen (albeit 5½in shorter), and they brought with them Det. Supt Maurice Osborn, who had a number of notable successes with the Yard's Murder Squad; in the latest, two men had been hanged five months earlier for murdering a farmer near Falmouth. 'A very nice guy, small in stature and a good cop,' was how John Strachan described him and Osborn's job was to instruct the office workers on how to collate and coordinate the evidence from the previous murder enquiries into what was known as The System. This meant the indexing and cross-indexing of not only names of witnesses but also details of everything and anything pertaining to the enquiry, including clothing, sightings, addresses and – car registration numbers. Just how complex *that* was to become, will later become apparent.

Jack Mannings, who had taken a proactive role in the Rees investigation, was there to provide his input and as he, Hatherill and Millen vanished from the scene, this left Det. Supt Bill Baldock, who was in charge of the CID of that area, and with Osborne as his deputy, he assumed overall charge – for now.

Like many of his contemporaries, Baldock had had his police service interrupted by the war, when he served with the Special Investigation Branch of the Military Police, but not before being awarded the British Empire Medal as a police constable for meritorious service in connection with war duties. He had served two tours with the Flying Squad and was a tremendous all-round copper, winning a total of nineteen commendations from the commissioner, the majority for the arrest of dangerous, armed and violent criminals. He was much admired and was referred to by Bob Cook as, 'that fine detective boss'. Bob Boyd described him, thus, 'He had a great presence, looked immaculate, tall, straight back and with his black hair and his black moustache he cut an impressive figure. He was typical of the good senior detectives of those days, they were respected.'

With such a multiplicity of talent, surely the days of this serial murderer were numbered? Well, that was the general idea.

★★★

Hatherill sent out an appeal for prostitutes who might have any information as to the killer's identity to contact Shepherd's Bush police station; and some did, although not with any intelligence that was especially pertinent to the investigation. It would be nice to think that both toms and 'tecs marched forward steadfastly in the relentless and united pursuit of the murderer but, alas, it would not be true. Incredibly, although prostitutes were the victims, many of them and their ponces used this as a heaven-sent opportunity to provide misinformation, lay false trails and to settle old scores.

There was far more interesting evidence surrounding the discovery of the latest victim, and especially on the body.

The corpse of Helene Catherine Barthelemy had been found on the morning of 24 April 1964 by Clark May. He went out of the back door of his home at 199 Boston Manor Road, Brentford, to empty some ashes and discovered the naked body on a rubbish tip outside his garden gate. It was a rear service road, off Swyncombe Avenue that, away from the fairly busy main thoroughfare, was a fairly deserted area, with a sports ground on one side of the road and playing fields on the other. The distance from the River Thames? About a mile. Coincidentally, as Mr May was telephoning the police, the body was also spotted by Christopher Parnell, an assistant groundsman at Beecham's Sports Ground, Acton, and he, too, had dialled 999.

When Donald Teare carried out the post-mortem at Acton mortuary later the same day, he deduced the victim had been dead for at least twenty-four hours, possibly a little longer. She had been strangled, possibly manually but probably by having her clothing twisted around her neck. There were abrasions on her throat and these were probably caused by Barthelemy fighting to remove the ligature. In addition there were swellings on her nose and cheekbone, administered before death, which were consistent with a punch. This was interesting; none of the other victims – with the possible exception of Tailford, who was definitely in the 'maybe – maybe not' category – had so far displayed signs of substantial violence, prior to their deaths. Perhaps Barthelemy had fought back; due to her former trade or calling in the circus, her work on a trapeze would have imbued her upper body with strength not normally associated with a woman and could have necessitated her attacker to disorientate her with punches to the face. Four of her teeth were missing – they had been removed after death – and the fragment of a tooth was found in her throat. Had there been any kind of sexual encounter with her attacker? Unlike the other victims, oral, vaginal and anal swabs were negative, although if there had been sexual contact, it is quite possible that a contraceptive had been used.

There were two matters of specific interest. The first was that hypostasis was present on her back; this was where blood congeals in a part of a body and it clearly showed the outline of her brassiere and panties, which revealed that, like her teeth, they had been removed after death – and of those (or any other items of clothing) there was no trace. And second, the body was filthy.

Initially, it was thought this was dirt, that the body had been left in an unclean, dusty area but there was far more to it than that. Initial scientific analysis revealed the material on the body was coal dust, plus various coloured paints, too small to be visible to the naked eye. Only when a microscope was used was it possible to see that the particles of paint measured between 10 and 50 microns; and to provide an idea as to how small that is, one micron measures 1-25,000th of an inch.

However, these paint deposits did not come from merely flicking a paintbrush; they were globular, such as might emerge from the nozzle of a spray gun. The most frequently found colour discovered on the body was black cellulose paint, ten times more common than the next, which was red. Therefore, garages that specialised in spraying cars – particularly London taxis – were suspect. However; bear in mind my usage of the term 'initial' when describing the analysis. It will surface again, later on.

And that apart, there was another very interesting line of enquiry. When Mr May had discovered the body, the time was 7.15 a.m. A neighbour had parked his car in that vicinity the previous evening at 10.55 p.m. and at that time, the body was not present. But an hour-and-a-half before the discovery of the body, there was a curious incident. Alfred Cecil Harrow was a smallholder from Denham, Buckinghamshire, and he was driving from his premises to Brentford Market along the Boston Manor Road, just as he had done, several times a week over the previous eight years. Almost as his van reached the junction with Swyncombe Avenue, a vehicle suddenly shot out of the avenue, causing Harrow to brake, swerve violently and stop. The offending vehicle, which Harrow believed was a grey Hillman Husky, did not stop, nor did the driver hesitate, look round nor show any kind of concern. Not that the driver appeared to be in any particular hurry – a Husky's acceleration from 0–60mph was a sluggish 26.9 seconds – but his vehicle did accelerate, as though he had just driven off. Harrow was unable to record the vehicle's registration number but in all the years he had travelled that route at that time he had never before seen that vehicle; however, when he read of the discovery of the body in the evening paper, he immediately associated the incident with the vehicle that had so narrowly missed him and he contacted the police. Since the junction where the collision had almost occurred was some 30 yards from where the body had been discovered, he was right to do so.

However, although Harrow kept a watchful eye open for the vehicle on his subsequent journeys to Brentford Market, he never saw it again; and neither did the plain-clothes officers who, for weeks on end, fruitlessly kept early morning vigils for it.

★★★

The press was full of the investigation and not just the British Press, either. *The Sunday Herald* from Provo, Utah, told its readers in the 26 April edition, 'Scotland Yard combed the Thames waterfront today in a search for the Brentford Strangler'. Two weeks later, West Germany's *Der Spiegel* described the common features of four of the murders, stating that, 'all four had grown small' although it's possible something came adrift in the translation. The popular newspaper from Lexington, North Carolina, *The Dispatch* (published daily, each afternoon, except Sunday) also informed its readers on 24 May of 'The Brentford Strangler' and stated, 'Constables on routine patrol in the foggy streets were ordered to pick up any loiterer whose actions seemed suspicious and bring him in for questioning'.

In fact, May 1964 was warm with slightly above normal sunshine with temperatures of 20°C–22°C but to the inhabitants of Lexington, NC, probably raised on a diet of Hollywood-produced Sherlock Holmes movies, the streets of Brentford had, of necessity, to be foggy.

While the investigation was carried out by a very limited number of officers, extra officers from outside the area were brought in to 'mind' certain prostitutes who were amenable to George Hatherill's warnings. One such officer was David Woodland who, with an aid to CID, would follow their designated prostitute – 'Maggie' – until she was picked up by a punter and follow his vehicle to Duke's Meadows or some other discreet venue, wait until the business had been transacted and see that she returned to her 'beat', usually in the Queensway area. 'It placed a heavy onus upon us,' he recalled, 'as the girls, placed in very real danger were effectively being used as live bait and it was a rather hit-and-miss affair.'

None of these matters were mentioned at Ealing Coroners' Court at the preliminary hearing on 27 April. The body was formerly identified to the coroner by her re-married mother, Mrs Mary Thomson of New Waltham, Grimsby, who told the court that she, 'had last seen her daughter about four years ago,' and Det. Supt Osborn asked for the inquest to be adjourned. *The Times* sombrely noted the police were continuing to 'search for the coloured man who, they believe, was the last person to see her alive'.

★★★

Helene Barthelemy had been born in East Lothian in 1941; her parents (father, French; mother, Scots) divorced and she travelled to Lancashire where, aged 16, she joined a circus as a trapeze artiste and then became a stripper along Blackpool's Golden Mile. Aged 18, she gave birth to a son, who was taken into care and later adopted, and she interspersed her duties as a stripper with soliciting prostitution – not that she was prosecuted for those offences.

However, she was prosecuted for robbery and unlawful wounding. On 27 July 1962, she met a 22-year-old man named Friend Taylor, who was on holiday at Blackpool. They arranged to meet at a hotel, where they spent some time together and then went to the sand hills at Quires Gate, where Taylor was viciously attacked by three men who repeatedly slashed his face with a sharp implement – a knife or a razor – and punched and kicked him. Taylor stated that Barthelemy shouted, 'Stop it, Jock – he's had enough.' and then the men – and Barthelemy – ran off, leaving Taylor badly slashed, having robbed him of £22 5s 0d. His wounds later required the insertion of eighteen stitches at Blackpool's Victoria Hospital.

Barthelemy was arrested the following day; her response to the allegations was a complete denial – she had not been at the scene, had never met Taylor and did not know his assailants. Unfortunately for her, she was identified, not only by Taylor but by several other independent witnesses who had seen them together prior to the attack and her alibi was not only as full of holes as a colander, it was found to be a pack of lies.

She appeared at Liverpool Assizes on 8 October, pleaded not guilty and said that at the time of the attack, she had gone to the cinema with another man and had spoken to the manager; she had indeed spoken to the cinema's manager, but this was on the night prior to the robbery. On the night that the offence took place, the manager told the court he was working in his office between 6.30 and 9.30 p.m. and therefore he could not have spoken to her; she was fortunate not to have been convicted of perjury.

After Barthelemy had been convicted of robbery on 10 October 1962 Mr Justice Stable sentenced her to four years' imprisonment.

On the facts, it was a just sentence for such an atrocious, premeditated crime; but everything was not as it seemed; and neither was Friend Taylor. He had been presented in a court as being a man of impeccable character, whereas nothing was further from the truth. He had two findings of guilt as a juvenile and four previous convictions for dishonesty; in fact, at the time of the assault on him, he had only recently been released from a twelve-month sentence for housebreaking.

Why had this not been mentioned in court? Surely the police must have checked up on his character – and if they did, they were duty-bound to inform the prosecution as well as defence team of this. If they did not check Taylor's antecedents, were they guilty of complete slovenliness in their duties? Almost certainly. If they were aware of his previous convictions, perhaps they thought that by admitting these matters to the defence, this would weaken the prosecution's case; but this was not necessarily so. Had the defence put Taylor's convictions to him, to show evidence of bad character, the prosecution would have been in a position to mention Barthelemy's conviction for assisting in the management of a brothel, for which she had been fined £20 at Liverpool City Magistrates' Court four months prior to the attack; and this would have done her case no good at all.

However, the court *did* become aware of Barthelemy's previous conviction, because she admitted it. Furthermore, she also told the jury that she was a prostitute and that following the fictitious outing to the cinema, she 'went on business' with three men, none of whom was Taylor. This was a daring defence, no error about that, but she really chanced her luck when she mentioned meeting four men from Preston earlier during the same month of the attack. Telling them that she was a prostitute, they suggested 'rolling a punter', a suggestion that she had no hesitation in haughtily rejecting. Asked in cross-examination if she knew what the term meant, she agreed that she knew exactly what it meant: robbing a customer. She added that she had never seen any of the men since that chance encounter but this account was rather spoiled after Friend Taylor gave evidence that he had seen Barthelemy talking to one of his attackers earlier in the day. The defence sounded quite unbelievable, as did her assertion that on the morning following the robbery, she had not visited the hairdressers with the intention of changing her appearance.

Whatever the circumstances, it resulted in the case being referred to the Court of Appeal (Criminal Division) before Mr Justice Ashworth, Mr Justice Winn and Mr Justice Lyell, in the following extraordinary circumstances. The trial judge, Mr Justice Stable, had granted a certificate for the appeal because he considered the case to be one 'of grave difficulty' and that the verdict should be considered by the Court of Appeal. He referred to his very long experience as a judge and described the case as one of the most puzzling he had ever had to try.

Precisely why the judge had experienced those misgivings is difficult to say; it appeared clear that Barthelemy had lied her head off in the witness box and when her alibi witness attempted to back up her story of them being elsewhere at the time of the attack, he was shown the statement he had previously made to the police that told a very different account of the evening. To rebut this, he stated that 'words were put into my mouth by the police' and that his signature had been prompted by the threats of physical violence.

It did not cause the jury the same confusion as it did the judge; they convicted Barthelemy after less than two hours' deliberations. It is only supposition but much of those two hours could have been spent in deliberating whether or not she was also guilty of unlawful wounding; they decided that she was not and acquitted her of that offence. It could well be that coming to the conclusion that Barthelemy was guilty of robbery took no time at all but who can second-guess the deliberations inside a jury room?

However, referring to Taylor's criminal record (which Mr Justice Ashworth described as 'disgraceful') it was felt that 'it was significant that it was not before the jury for it was evidence that might have swayed the jury'. This was sufficient to overturn the verdict and on 4 February 1963 Barthelemy was released.

She had been represented by James Comyn, QC (later Sir James and a high court judge), who would go on to successfully appear for Alfie Hinds, the celebrated safe-blower, who was then serving twelve years' preventative detention, in a libel case against the police. Although Hinds won the case, he was certainly guilty, as was Barthelemy, but in her case there was little enough for Comyn to do.

It raises a point; had the police obtained Friend's convictions at the time of the trial and was the prosecution aware of them? The Crown was led by Brian Roy Duckworth, later His Honour Judge Duckworth DL, MA who at the time of his death in 2014 had been the country's longest serving circuit judge. And it was Duckworth who appeared for the Crown at the Court of Appeal, where the senior judge remarked, 'Mr Duckworth has very properly informed the court that the victim has a criminal record.' But when was Duckworth aware of it? Before Barthelemy's trial? During it? Immediately afterwards? And did he mention this fact to Mr Justice Stable, which would certainly have given rise to the 'grave difficulty' he had experienced when he referred the matter to the Court of Appeal? All a matter of conjecture, of course, and one that now will never be resolved.

By freeing her from what many would feel was a conviction and sentence that was fully justified, the Court of Appeal had unconsciously condemned Helene Barthelemy to death; but such are the vagaries of British justice.

★★★

Within months, Barthelemy had moved to London, sometimes calling herself Teddy and using the aliases Helen Paul (the name of a former land-lady) and Helen Thompson (her mother's re-married name), she lived at

34 Talbot Road, Harlesden. From there she roamed the streets over a wide area, soliciting prostitution from punters in cars, often going to the area of Duke's Meadows. Just 5ft 1in tall, a pretty girl with an attractive figure, she was a natural brunette who sometimes dyed her hair red. In between times, she sought the attention of black men and, it was rumoured, white women, both for recreational purposes, and often visited The Roaring Twenties nightclub in Carnaby Street (as did Irene Lockwood, together with her black ponce of three years' standing). It was an out of control establishment where drugs were peddled and smoked and Barthelemy was fortunate to escape the attention of DS Harry Challenor MM from West End Central police station, who was prone to raid the club on the slightest pretext and who was just as out of control as the establishment.

Barthelemy was one of the many prostitutes to be warned by the police to look out for themselves, just a few days before her death; unfortunately, she failed to heed this advice and she was seen at her home address on 21 April at 8.30 p.m., just over two days before her body was discovered. That sighting and the time and date are a certainty.

However, the waters became a little muddied because as well as frequenting The Roaring Twenties, Barthelemy also patronised The Jazz Club at 207 Westbourne Park Road, Notting Hill. It was possible that she was seen there, thirty-six hours after being seen at her home address, at two o'clock on the morning of 23 April, when she may have left her handbag there and it was later handed to the police. However, so much dope was being smoked and the statements of the witnesses so imprecise that, while there was no doubt Barthelemy did at some time leave her handbag in the club, precisely when that was would be open to doubt.

It was thought that she was last seen wearing a brown topcoat with a black leather collar, a black jumper with a high neck, a tight skirt and black leather boots. Several of her black boyfriends were questioned (this included the one to whom *The Times* had referred); none of them could throw any light on her demise and not a few admitted they had 'no idea' that she was a prostitute – this to absolve themselves of being branded her ponce. At the time of her death she was infected with gonorrhoea (as were several of her boyfriends) and if she did not enjoy anal sex it was provided for at least some of her clients.

Although the police had fingerprinted Barthelemy's room and traced all the owners of those prints – and eliminated them from the enquiry – the fact remained that she had been killed, stripped, her body stored somewhere where the globules of paint, almost certainly airborne, had settled on her naked body and then taken by some form of vehicle to the dumping ground

It seemed to have been a hurried disposal. The murderer had not previously taken a body so far away from what was later to be found to be the storage place before abandoning it. That morning, dawn had broken at 5.44 a.m. and the murderer had left himself little or no time to get far away from the scene to avoid discovery; the arrival of daylight coincided exactly with the hurried departure in the vehicle that was witnessed by Alfred Harrow.

At Ealing Coroners' Court on 2 November 1964, after enquires lasting more than six months, Det. Supt Osborn told the inquest jury, 'She associated with coloured people quite a lot, probably drug addicts.' Since the Race Relations Act was still a year away from being placed on the statute books, this comment was probably sufficient to send a shiver through the middle-class, home-owning jurors who, having been told by the coroner, Dr Harold Broadbridge, 'The police are up against a brick wall,' returned a verdict of 'murder by a person or persons unknown'.

But prior to this, a senior reporter at the now defunct *News of the World* wrote a very odd piece for the 19 July edition of the Sunday newspaper. It was in the form of an open letter designed, one supposes, to oblige the killer to give himself up and report, tear-stained and penitent at his nearest police station, clutching a signed confession. However, it was couched in such contemptuous, patronising terms with the astonishing passages containing the words, 'Perhaps you can't help yourself when, in the midst of your obscenities with a cheap, bought woman, the red mist comes down and your hands tighten and tighten and tighten. Perhaps, when you are caught, they will save you from the searing rope because you are ill, sick in your mind.' And later, 'I know the type of women you favour. All your victims have been scrubbers, cheap little tarts, pepped up by fifty purple heart tablets a day to perform unspeakable perversions with any man who pulls up in a car and has £1 in his pocket.'

It is quite likely that upon reading these words (and many more like them) the killer would have ignored the final paragraph to 'Ring Detective

Superintendent Maurice Osborn at Shepherds Bush 1113 and get it all over – NOW' since this would have whipped him into a frenzy to kill again.

In fact, he would and following the murder of Barthelemy, he already had; five days before the publication of the article the body of Mary Fleming had been found.

VICTIM NO. 6

MARY FLEMING

Mary Fleming was found lying in the entrance to a garage at 48 Berrymead Road, Chiswick, at 4.45 on the morning of 14 July 1964. George Heard, a chauffeur who lived opposite, had got up early because his daughter was going on a day trip to France. He looked out of his bedroom window to see what he thought initially was a tailor's dummy in his neighbour's driveway. When he realised that the curled up, naked figure was human – and dead – he called the police.

The body – 5ft 1½in tall – was removed to Hammersmith mortuary, where Donald Teare carried out the autopsy. Once again, there was evidence of hypostasis; the body had been stripped after death and once more, abrasions on the neck suggested the victim had clawed at the ligature – again, possibly her own clothing – as she was strangled. This time, matters were slightly different, in that, as in the case of Barthelemy, there were signs of physical violence. A large bruise just above her heart suggested a very hard punch, indeed. Had Fleming struggled in the same way as Barthelemy may have done? Or had the killer thought that she might? There was also a bruise on her coccyx together with grease marks on her buttocks that corresponded with oil in the road just outside the murder scene, suggesting she had been dragged from a car to the driveway. A vaginal swab proved positive. She had used a denture and that, together with her clothing and handbag, was missing. The body was slightly less the distance from the Thames as Barthelemy's had been – about three-quarters of a mile.

The occupier of No. 48 was questioned and was able to say that when he had gone to bed at 11.30 the previous evening the body was not there. However, neighbours had heard a vehicle reversing later in the early hours of that morning. Berrymead Road was a cul-de-sac; entry and exit to it was made via Acton Lane, although access to it could also be made via Priory Road and Saville Road.

In addition, at about 2.20 that morning, two men, John Francis Boyle and William Vincent Kirwin, were busily painting the interior of the ABC Restaurant in Chiswick High Road when they heard the sound of a vehicle being reversed and car doors being slammed. They looked out of the restaurant's rear windows to see a vehicle – perhaps a small grey van or an estate – in the car park. There was a man standing beside it but, although they were unable to describe him or provide a registration number for the vehicle, they nevertheless recalled that they called out facetiously to him, perhaps to startle him. If that was their intention, they succeeded; the man looked at them, got quickly into the vehicle and drove off, turning right from the car park and into Acton Lane.

The significance of this is that the restaurant was a ten-minute drive away from Berrymead Road, a turning off Acton Lane and less than three-quarters of a mile away; and it was at about 2.30 that residents in Berrymead Road heard the sounds of a vehicle reversing. Was this the same vehicle that Messrs' Boyle and Kirwin saw? And if it was, did the vehicle contain the body of Fleming? Had the driver intended to dump the corpse in the car park of – what he obviously thought was – the deserted restaurant, panicked and then deposited the body in the cul-de-sac? It seems practically inescapable that this was the case and – this is important – panicking or not, he had a sufficient knowledge of the region to know the second of two deserted areas.

The witness in the Barthelemy case had been involved in the near collision with what he believed to be a grey Hillman Husky. The vehicle probably used in the Fleming murder and seen by the painters was also grey – it could have been a Hillman Husky but it could also have been a Commer Cob, introduced early in 1956, which was very similar in appearance to a Husky.

By plotting these events in chronological sequence, it seems almost certain that the two sightings of these vehicles in the Barthelemy and Fleming cases were one and the same; unfortunately – and this would happen several times during the investigation – the information from the painters was not reported immediately. If it had, the link between the two vehicle sightings would have dovetailed straight away. However, it did not emerge until months later when the connection was made, following the huge wave of publicity.

Hillman Huskys were first brought into production in 1954; in the first three years alone, 42,000 were sold until the new model commenced in 1958. While this enquiry was under way, they were still coming off the production line and would continue to do so until the enquiry closed. Undeniably, this would have been the perfect vehicle to transport a corpse. A two-door estate, the bench seat at the back could be folded down and access to the rear was provided by a single, side-hinged door. Best of all, it was an unremarkable looking vehicle and a neutral colour; with so many of them on the roads, it was pretty well anonymous.

Therefore, it was decided to make a thorough and painstaking search through the registration authorities to trace the registered owners and/or drivers of all Hillman Huskys and Commer Cobs that were in use during April to July 1964, when the bodies of Barthelemy and Fleming had been found.

Nowadays, the computer at the DVLC would be tapped into for the details of the registered keepers of all of these vehicles and the details would be made available within minutes; checking them out would take rather longer, of course. However, that was not the case in 1964. These details, kept in card indices at the London and Middlesex County Councils, were not in make or model of vehicle order; they were kept in consecutive registration numbers, a number the murder squad did not possess. It meant that every single card, of every single vehicle – cars, motorcycles, vans, lorries and coaches – had to be checked. At Middlesex details of 600,000 vehicles were housed and at the London County Council, more than 1 million others. Could matters get any worse? Yes, they could. With the best will in the world, the registration authorities simply did not have enough staff to carry out such a monumental undertaking; therefore, police officers would have to be used. Initially, six women police constables (later increased to eleven) under the direction of a detective sergeant, set to work.

And if that were not enough, with the birth of the Greater London Council, it meant the amalgamation of the motor registration records, not only of the London and Middlesex County Councils, but also those of Croydon Borough Council, East and West Ham Councils and also parts of Essex, Hertfordshire and Surrey registration authorities. With masterly understatement, Baldock described it as, 'a formidable task'.

So apart from the fact that Fleming and Barthelemy worked the same area and both had contracted gonorrhoea, together with the other similarities of their deaths, Fleming, too had the minute particles of paint on her skin that corresponded with those found on Barthelemy; after death, both had been stored in the same place.

★★★

Fleming had been born Mary Theresa Cuthbertson Betty at Dumbarton in 1933 and twenty years later she married James Fleming. The marriage floundered during her husband's National Service with the Royal Army Medical Corps in Germany and during the next ten years she gave birth to four children. Of the first two – both boys – the first was dumped on her parents, the second was put into care. She arrived in London in 1956 and acquired her first conviction when she was 23 for soliciting prostitution in Stepney's Commercial Road; for this she was bound over to be of good behaviour. The following month she was convicted again, for the same offence. She was fined three more times in 1957, two for offences of soliciting, another for committing an act of indecency.

In 1958, having stolen property that belonged to her landlord, she fled to Scotland, where she industriously helped herself to the contents of her relatives' gas meters. Returning to London, she was arrested for the offence against her landlord and, having appeared in court, was conditionally discharged. Fleming must, by now, have believed that she could commit whatever offences she liked with impunity. However, this proved not to be the case when, in 1959, she was convicted of stealing £5 3s 0d from the gas meter at her lodgings and she came down to earth with a bump when she was sentenced to three months' imprisonment.

A bump figured prominently when she was convicted for the eighth (and final) time for soliciting prostitution in 1961, because she was once more pregnant; it probably acted as mitigation for her, because she was placed on probation.

Now, prematurely old at 31, her looks fading fast, her body slack and unattractive, only the most credulous of her listeners paid any heed to her stories of being paid a fortune to attend deviant Mayfair parties.

She drifted from flat to flat, each one a dump; her on-off boyfriend provided her with two more children and their relationship came to an abrupt halt after he went to their flat in Powis Gardens, Notting Hill, to find their daughter, almost a year old, on her own. Having a fairly good idea where she might be, he went straight round to The Jazz Club (whose alumni had included Helene Barthelemy) and found Fleming drunk, dancing with a black man; during the inevitable ensuing altercation, the police were called.

The next port of call was a flat in Geraldine Road, Chiswick, where among the disparate tenants was a prostitute imaginatively named Gloria Swanson (not to be confused with the Hollywood star of the same name who had appeared in so many of Cecil B. DeMille's films and who, at 65 years of age, was looking rather more glamorous than her exotically named West London counterpart who was thirty years her junior).

Whatever money Fleming made, she spent largely on herself, buying cigarettes, alcohol and amphetamines. At the time of her death, a summons, returnable to West London Magistrates' Court, had been served on her alleging the forging of documents in order to claim public assistance. By now, owing rent at Geraldine Road, she and her two children, aged two and eight months were living in a one-bedroom flat at 44 Lancaster Road, Notting Hill, which she had adroitly managed to turn into a revolting tip.

'Gloria Swanson' last saw Fleming on the evening of 10 July when Fleming told her she intended to go out, 'for a gay time and felt like getting drunk'. In the early hours of the following morning she met a couple of young prostitutes whom she knew and who were window shopping. They chatted casually until Fleming remarked, 'I'm going to earn some money.' Shortly afterwards she encountered one of the police officers patrolling the streets in an effort to 'mind' the prostitutes. She took a knife out of her handbag and told the officer, 'I know how to use this; you don't have to worry about me.' The officer disregarded this breach of the Prevention of Crimes Act, 1953 that, with hindsight was a mistake. The penalty of three months in quod would have been a good result for Mrs Fleming; whether she was expert in the use of a knife or not, it failed to save her.

The last time she was seen alive was by a member of the British Transport Police in the Bayswater Road at 2.45 on the morning of 11 July, getting out of a red Volkswagen. She was then wearing a blue and white heavy woollen fawn check, two-piece costume and her cheap white plastic shoes complemented her black and white handbag; but they were all missing when her naked body was discovered three days later. Did that handbag contain a pawn ticket that had been issued to Fleming two weeks previously, when she had pawned a ladies watch in return for £2 1s 6d? If it did, nobody ever redeemed the pledge; and no trace of the ticket was ever found.

★★★

The press immediately latched on to the murder, with the *Daily Mirror*'s edition of 15 July proclaiming 'Nude No 5 – River Killer Hunted' and now, courtesy of the United States press, it was possibly the first time that the *nom de guerre*, 'Jack the Stripper' was used. It came from *The Dispatch* (Davidson County's News Source), the same day as the *Daily Mirror*'s story and also stated that Det. Supt Maurice Osborn urged prostitutes, 'to stay out of strangers' cars and co-operate with the police'. And the following day, Connecticut's *The Bridgeport Telegraph* also adopted the nickname, telling its readers, 'Prostitutes are quizzed on Jack the Stripper'.

One week after his promotion and transfer to 'F' Division from his second of two tours with the Flying Squad, Det. Supt Bill Marchant walked straight into this murder. A former captain with the Royal Sussex Regiment, 47-year-old Marchant was married with five children and was a highly astute investigator who had worked with the Yard's highly secretive post-war Ghost Squad. Now, Marchant joined forces with Maurice Osborn.

From the two promising leads, the sighting of the suspect grey vehicles and the paint-impregnated bodies of the victims, far more personnel would be required than the present numbers of officers. Assistant

Commissioner (Crime) Sir Ranulph 'Rasher' Bacon KPM was consulted. One of Commissioner Lord Trenchard's pre-war 'officer class', Sir Ranulph had risen through the ranks to be appointed ACC in 1963; he was much admired as an administrator. Yes, it was clear more officers would be needed to supplement this enquiry but matters were not as clear cut as all that.

In 1912, 20,529 officers – 639 of them detectives – policed the capital, which had a population of 7,393,969 that reported 17,519 crimes. By 1964, the number of officers had increased slightly by 251 to 20,780 and the number of detectives had almost tripled, to 1,871. They were needed; the population had increased to 8,186,830 and the number of reported crimes had shot up to 254,260 – an increase of 25,153 from the previous year – and almost fifteen times the statistics of 1912. In fact, 1964 was the worst year for reported crimes thus far in the twentieth century; there were also 223 fewer officers than the previous year. The Regional Crime Squads were formed to cover all England and Wales and were tasked with co-ordinating investigations into cross-border crime, especially lorry hijackings and burglaries, although this was funded separately by the Home Office. So was the Metropolitan Police and every penny of its £53,812,228 annual budget was being scrutinised.

It all made a pretty convincing argument for the Met's budget to be increased to £59,741,414 the following year (plus an increase in manpower by another 4,278 officers) especially since the crime statistics would increase by another 21,744. However, for now Sir Ranulph had to do with what he'd got – and officers from other divisions (who could ill afford to spare them) were drafted in to assist with this enquiry.

Fleming's inquest was held, together with Barthelemy's, at Ealing Coroners' Court on 2 November 1964; the jury's verdict on both was recorded by the coroner, Dr Harold Broadbridge, as being 'murder by a person or persons unknown' and Fleming was buried the following day; Barthelemy had been buried six weeks earlier.

Night-duty patrols were stepped up. Prostitutes – they nervously or contemptuously referred to the killer as 'a goon' or 'a maniac'– and their ponces were being questioned, all to no avail. A staff of sixty was employed at the Metropolitan Police Forensic Laboratory since dust samples – in excess of 150 – from garages and boots of cars that had been collected on sticky tape were being forwarded to them. The reasoning was clear; find the source of the contamination found on the bodies of Barthelemy and Fleming and the case – indeed, *all* the cases – would be solved.

The Fleming investigation alone had been going on for more than four months. Hundreds of statements had been taken; hundreds of car registration numbers had been noted, the drivers questioned, dust samples obtained. Were the police getting close to a breakthrough?

Not a bit of it. The next murder victim's body – that of Frances Brown – was found on 25 November 1964. And again, the killer had differed from the norm. This time, his latest victim had been buried.

VICTIM NO. 7

FRANCES BROWN

The murderer could not be unaware of the furore that his activities had caused; admittedly, not all the Metropolitan Police's 20,780 officers were engaged actively in the search for him but a significant proportion of them were and it would be a very large feather in the cap of the officer who laid hands on him. But no one had. He had taken on the might of Scotland Yard and, in the same small area of London, he had done it again. He had also changed his tactics. The bodies of Barthelemy and Fleming had been subjected to violence as well as being found approximately a mile away from the Thames. If we discount the case of Gwynneth Rees, this was the first time an attempt had been made to bury the body. It could only have been intended to prevent a quick discovery of the body, as had happened on the previous occasions. Furthermore, care had been taken to select a spot for dumping the body, some distance from the other victims. It was unfortunate that the body was not discovered for five weeks, a period that could not possibly have been anticipated by the murderer, since only a dustbin lid covered the dead woman's head in a very busy car park in Kensington.

It was as though the killer was privy to the tactics used by police. Of course, he would be aware of the police investigation in all of the cases because of the amount of press coverage and therefore he would be conscious of extra numbers of police being deployed in the areas where the victims had both been picked up, and dumped – hence the change in his procedures. However, it was clear he was cunning – it was equally obvious that he was as mad as a box of frogs – as well as having a shrewd, analytical mind.

And yet it seemed that the killer had no fear of getting caught. The last hangings in England had taken place three months earlier, although there were six categories of murder that still attracted the death penalty, including – and especially pertinent to this case – the second of two murders committed on different occasions if both had been carried out in Great Britain. But not for much longer; on 21 December, MPs voted 355 to 170 for the abolition of the death penalty for murder, which was suspended in Parliament in 1965 and made permanent in 1969.

Between the time of her last being seen by fellow prostitute Kim Taylor on 23 October 1964 and the body of Frances Brown being found, over a month had lapsed. On 25 November at the Civil Defence Headquarters at Phillimore Walk, just off Kensington High Street, Dennis Sutton, the assistant Civil Defence officer saw a dustbin lid on the ground at the rear of the Hornton Street car park, which he recognised as belonging to a dustbin at his headquarters. He lifted it only to discover what was left of a woman's face underneath and after the police and the pathologist were called, a shallow grave, made up from local debris was removed to find the rest of her badly decomposed body, which was infested with maggots. The use of a dustbin lid to cover the victim's face seemed almost symbolic; it was as though the murderer was contemptuously saying, 'Look what's under this dustbin lid – it's rubbish.'

The autopsy was far from easy but the findings were depressingly similar to the other victims. Brown had been asphyxiated with abrasions on the throat consistent with the victim attempting to remove the cause of the pressure. She possibly suffered from venereal disease, three of her teeth were missing and hypostasis revealed that she had been stripped after death. Her clothing, jewellery and handbag were missing and were never found. A piece of plain paper was stuffed into her vagina. And, of course, there were paint samples on the body that were a close match to those found on the bodies of the previous two victims.

The nearest police station, Kensington, was used as the base for this latest investigation, and Bill Marchant took over the running of this enquiry as well.

Delving into her background, he discovered that Brown had been born in 1943 in Glasgow – and that subsequently, she would also be known as Margaret McGowan, Anne and also Donna Sutherland, Susan Edwards, Nuala Rowlands and lately, Frances Quinn. Her first brush with the law came at the tender age of 11 when she was placed on probation for larceny. In and out of approved school, she had three illegitimate children and collected her first of several convictions for soliciting prostitution in London when she was 18. Aged 29, she was convicted at Glasgow Sheriffs' Summary Court for child neglect and was placed on probation for two years. Six months later she was sectioned under the Mental Health Act and in between times moved in with a Paul Quinn, five years her senior and the possessor of a varied criminal record. A common bond between the two of them was that he had served prison sentences and she was just about to serve one.

In November 1963, she appeared at Marylebone Magistrates' Court and for attempting to steal a car she was given the option of being fined £10 or one month's imprisonment. Obviously impecunious, she chose the latter; Quinn (he was also known as Pepe) later paid the fine but following her release she was rearrested and sentenced to three months' imprisonment for child neglect at Glasgow Sheriffs' Court. She returned to London and at the time of her disappearance, Brown and Quinn were living in a flat at Southerton Road, Hammersmith, with her baby, Frank. During the course of the enquiry, three matters came to light.

★★★

The first was the scandal that rocked the nation involving John Profumo and Stephen Ward. Briefly, John Dennis Profumo, the Secretary of State for War, who was much admired in the House and who had a brilliant war record had, in July 1961, despite being married to the beautiful film star, Valerie Hobson, unwisely started a sexual relationship with a 19-year-old model named Christine Keeler. It was a short-lived affair but details of it were known to the security services since Keeler had also had an affair with Captain Yevgeni Ivanov, an assistant naval attaché at the Russian Embassy and also a member of the Glavnoye Razvedyvatel'noye Upravleniye (GRU), or the Soviet foreign military intelligence directorate. To add to this unwise mix came Stephen Ward, an osteopath with consulting rooms at Devonshire Street, W1, a flat at Wimpole Mews, W1, and a country cottage on the Cliveden Estate, the country seat of Lord Astor, which was where Profumo and Keeler had met. Ward had an eye for attractive young girls – some of whom he seduced and passed on to his friends – possessed a collection of pornographic photographs and attended parties where, according to Lord Denning, 'there were sexual orgies of a revolting nature.' And in addition, Ward, who admired the Soviet regime, was very friendly with Ivanov.

It was a matter that could have been dealt with discreetly had it not been for the fact that in October 1962 there was a fight at the All-Nighters' club in Soho's Wardour Street in which Aloysius 'Lucky' Gordon, a friend of Keeler's, was slashed in the face, necessitating seventeen stiches. Later, a number of shots were fired from an automatic pistol at Ward's flat in Wimpole Mews, where the one of the occupants at that time was Keeler. Another was Ward's friend Marilyn 'Mandy' Rice-Davies, also the mistress of Perec 'Peter' Rachman, the notorious, Polish-born slum landlord of Notting Hill who had been twice prosecuted for brothel-keeping. As a result of the shooting, another paramour of Keeler's, Johnnie Edgecombe, was arrested and charged with both the slashing and the shooting.

Keeler sold her story to the *Sunday Pictorial* for £1,000 (which was then almost a year's wages for a semi-skilled worker) and also produced incriminating letters written to her by Profumo. Ward contacted the police, stating that certain photographs had been stolen from him and that the whole matter 'might bring down the Government'.

In the meantime, Edgecombe's trial started on 14 March 1963; there was no trace of Keeler, a very important witness for the prosecution, and the next day there were banner headlines in the *Daily Express*, 'War Minister Shock' in which Profumo stated that he would not resign – 'There is no reason why I should' – and while Edgecombe was acquitted of four charges (including the slashing of 'Lucky' Gordon) he was convicted of possessing a firearm with intent to endanger life. He had a varied and interesting criminal record: convicted of larceny on two occasions in 1951, living on immoral earnings in 1959 and, three years later, possession of dangerous drugs, Edgecombe was now sent down for seven years. Ward sold his own version of events to the

Sunday Pictorial and on 22 March Profumo made a statement to the House, denying any impropriety in his relationship with Keeler.

Matters now moved very quickly. On 1 April, police started investigating the activities of Ward. Seventeen days later, Keeler was allegedly attacked by her former boyfriend, 'Lucky' Gordon, and he was arrested. On 5 June, Gordon came up for trial; on the same day, Profumo admitted lying to Parliament and resigned. Two days later, Gordon was convicted of actual body harm and was sentenced to three years' imprisonment. The next day, 8 June, Ward was arrested and charged with living on the earnings of prostitution of Keeler, Rice-Davies and Vickie Barrett, and the day after that the *Sunday Mirror* published a copy of Profumo's letter to Keeler. On the same day, the *News of the World* started publishing Keeler's story in instalments – she was paid £23,000 for it. It did her little good; at Gordon's successful appeal, it was revealed that Keeler had lied on oath and in December 1963 she was sentenced to nine months' imprisonment for perjury.

Ward's trial commenced at the Old Bailey on 22 July 1963 and on 30 July the judge started his summing up. Despite police objections, Ward had been on £3,000 bail throughout the trial and the following day, he was admitted to hospital suffering from an overdose of Nembutal. The judge continued his summing up, the jury found Ward guilty of living on the immoral earnings of Keeler and Rice-Davies and the case was adjourned until Ward was recovered sufficiently to reappear. He never did. Ward died on 3 August without recovering consciousness, which as Noël Coward observed in his diary, 'was very sensible of him'.

The whole matter received the widest, most salacious publicity that titillated wildly the imagination of the great British public. There were stories of well-known figures being whipped by prostitutes and when it was suggested that eight high court judges were involved simultaneously in a sex orgy, a dazed Prime Minister, Harold Macmillan, muttered to a colleague, 'Two, conceivably, but eight! I just can't believe it.' The names of the great and the good were mentioned, including Lord Astor, the painter and sculptor Vasco Lazzolo and – furiously denied – the actor Douglas Fairbanks Jr., KBE, DSC. However, the fact remained that national security was not breached, Profumo's wife stood solidly by him and Profumo devoted himself to charitable works that were recognised in 1975 with the award of Commander of the British Empire when he was brought back in from the cold. However, Ward's prophesy proved gloomily correct; this case was one of the contributory factors that brought down the government.

The relevance of this is that Frances Brown gave evidence for the defence in Ward's case. The third charge that Ward had been facing was living on the immoral earnings of one Vicky Barrett (her baptismal name was Janet Barker), a prostitute with whom Brown often solicited, and after reading Barrett's steamy testimony for the prosecution in the newspapers (beating men with a horsewhip while attired in underwear and high heels) Brown came to court 'to put the record straight'.

Apparently, Quinn was furious at her actions; in giving evidence, she would have to admit that she was a prostitute and by imputation it would therefore appear that he was her ponce – which, of course was quite true. He later admitted to the press, 'I lived off her earnings as a prostitute from 1962.'

Barrett had told the court that, among other acts, she had had sexual relations with the artist, Lazzolo; he had appeared as a defence witness to say that nothing of the kind had occurred. However, in endeavouring to 'put the record straight', Brown told the court that not only had there been a sexual encounter between Barrett and Lazzolo, she had been present when it happened and, as she put it, 'I helped'. (In his supercilious account of the trial, Ludovic Kennedy suggested that these words should be engraved upon Brown's tombstone. When his book was published one week after the discovery of Brown's body, I wonder if he had a pang of conscience? No, probably not.) Barrett had also told the court she had not had sexual intercourse with Stephen Ward; Brown said she had, since she had been present as an observer and Ward agreed that he and Barrett had had sexual relations – but he made no mention of Brown being there.

The waters had been spectacularly muddied with a number of witnesses, both for the prosecution and the defence lying their heads off, but by coming forward it appears that Brown was successful, inasmuch as Ward was acquitted of the charge in respect of Barrett. (It was also suggested in the press that Brown arrived at the hospital with flowers for Ward but was unkindly turned away; true or not, it added a touch of verisimilitude to the whole unhappy affair.)

So why did Brown, an inveterate liar with mental health issues, come forward and travel the 131 miles from Smethwick in the West Midlands to London to give evidence for a man who, if she was to be believed, she had only met twice and had never been intimate with? The short answer is 'publicity'; and that was true – every prostitute who gave evidence got their picture in the paper.

This was, in part, corroborated by the trial judge, Mr Justice Marshall who, in his summing up told the jury, 'The widespread and exaggerated publicity surrounding this trial has brought these girls to pinnacles of notoriety which feed and fan their vanity.'

However, if Brown thought her revelations were going to sweep her up into the sensational world of the glitterati who featured in the Ward case, she was to be sadly mistaken. Anybody – friend or foe – who had anything to do with Ward were busy rowing for the shore. The deviations of the upper classes had been a shared secret between them. Now, it was out in the open and they had no time for a tattooed tom who was a drunk, a liar and a drug addict with a multitude of aliases, and whom they left to less discerning company – which included her killer.

All this had been largely forgotten, except that the press suddenly put two and two together, two days after the discovery of Brown's body: 'Nude No 6 was Stephen Ward Witness' were the *Daily Mirror's* headlines, together with a photograph of her. Suddenly, speculation was rife; Hannah Tailford had been involved in 'kinky parties' – had she also involved with Ward? And Brown had been friendly with Helene Barthelemy – and also Mary Fleming – was there a link there? All this provided Bill Marchant with coverage he could have well done without. John du Rose would later say that the investigating team questioned all the witnesses in the Ward case, although given the mass of other work that was generated, this is unlikely; and what was more, any connection between the Ward case and the death of Brown was not just unlikely, it was ludicrous.

The usual and predictable band of conspiracy theorists decided that the security services had murdered Brown for daring to go against the establishment. Quite apart from the fact that MI5 has always steadfastly maintained that it does not carry out assassinations on British soil (and to paraphrase Mandy Rice-Davis, 'Well, they would, wouldn't they?') the idea is absurd.

If it were true, because the murders had been linked, it would mean the government assassin would also have murdered the previous victims before even knowing that Brown was going to give evidence in the Ward trial, as well as additionally murdering the next victim.

★★★

The second of the two matters was something very odd that has never been resolved satisfactorily. Frances Brown kept in intermittent contact with her mother, Helen Brown, who lived in Glasgow and in mid-September 1964 Mrs Brown received an enthusiastic, newsy letter from her daughter informing her of their new address in Hammersmith. Mrs Brown obviously responded to the letter because she received a postcard, depicting Piccadilly Circus, dated 1 October 1964, which read:

> Dear Mom,
> I received your letter ok Paul
> myself & Baby are doing fine and I hope all
> is the same at home
> Lots of love
> Frances

The postcard was puzzling in three respects: Frances always referred to her mother as Ma or Mammy – not Mom. Second, she would address letters to her mother giving the Gallowgate address as 'Glasgow' not 'Scotland' as had been the case with this postcard. And lastly, Mrs Brown would later say that the writing on the postcard was nothing like her daughter's handwriting.

It was not as if Brown had been murdered at that time; that would occur almost three weeks later. And if she had not written the postcard – and it appears quite likely that she did not – who did? And for what reason?

★★★

And lastly, a promising lead came from Kim Taylor, alias Beryl Mahood, Brown's fellow prostitute; Taylor had apparently shared a flat with Vicky

Barrett. After Brown's body was discovered, she told the police that on the evening of 23 October 1964, she and Brown had left the Warwick Castle pub when they had been picked up by two men in two separate cars, who were obviously known to each other, by the junction with Portobello Road and Westbourne Park Road. Brown suggested she and Taylor travel in one of the cars to the Chiswick Green area with the other man following on behind but it was decided that the two women would travel in separate cars. Brown got into what might have been a Ford Zephyr with a man described as being aged between 30 and 35, about 5ft 8in tall with dark brown hair with a full face. He was wearing a suede jacket with a white sheepskin or lambswool collar. They drove off, followed by Taylor and her companion, but they lost the first car in traffic and ended up having sexual intercourse in a car park. Taylor described her companion as being 5ft 10in, medium build and aged between 30 and 32. He had thinning brown hair and a round face, full lips and slightly protruding ears. He was driving a new, light grey car with a bench front seat and a column gear change and made a date with her at the Warwick Castle pub the following Wednesday. He seemed unconcerned about losing sight of his companion, saying that 'he knew where to find him at the flat'. Taylor's client dropped her off but that was the last she saw of Brown, who was wearing a green two-piece suit with a fur collar, a white blouse and black suede shoes.

Taylor compiled an identikit picture of the two men, which was issued to the press on 4 December, but neither of the men were ever identified. The police believed the men may have been attending the Earl's Court motor show, which was being held the night they picked up the two prostitutes and also on the following Friday, 30 October. An appeal was made on the popular television programme, *Police 5* and then, shortly afterwards, an inquest was held on 24 February 1965 at Hammersmith Coroners' Court. After hearing from the witnesses, especially the pathologist Donald Teare who informed the court that the cause of death was asphyxiation, caused by pressure to the neck, a verdict of death by a person or persons unknown was recorded.

However, matters could not be simply left there. In fact, on 27 February 1965, it was decided to reissue the image of the man who had gone off with Brown. At that time, Taylor was in custody in Accrington, Lancashire, charged with larceny. That case was dismissed and at the enquiry team's request she came to Shepherd's Bush police station on 4 March to give any further assistance she could; in fact, she was able to provide information regarding the perverted practices and associates of Brown. Additionally, she was helpful in making contacts with many of the prostitutes who worked the west London area and without her assistance it is extremely unlikely that these girls would have come forward. But despite Taylor accompanying police in the Bayswater, Shepherd's Bush and Notting Hill areas, she was unable to identify the two men whom she and Brown had encountered on the night Brown disappeared.

Despite Taylor's helpfulness, matters may not have been as straightforward as described. On the day of Brown's disappearance, both women had been drinking heavily in the Warwick Castle pub from noon onwards; four months later, Taylor would tell the inquest that Brown had drunk about eight whiskeys and cokes during the afternoon and approximately eleven whiskeys in the evening; and yet the post-mortem had revealed no more than the equivalent of two to three measures of spirits in her stomach. It is quite possible that Taylor was accompanying Brown drink for drink – whatever that consumption was – and that this could have affected her memory.

And next, Taylor did not speak to the police until 27 November, more than a month after Brown had disappeared; and much would have happened during that time in a busy prostitute's life. It was then that she compiled the identikit pictures and now there is a line of thought she may have been confused as to which of the two women got into which car with which man. Having done that, the matters became somewhat clouded when, four days after her meeting with the police, Taylor gave a lurid version of the events to the *Evening Standard*, which included an account of how, on 30 November, two men in a van had tried to run her down. The following week, Taylor repeated her story to the *News of the World* and the week after that there was a further story of how she was attacked by a man who warned her to 'keep her trap shut' as she left a west London jazz club.

Was all of this the unvarnished truth – or were there elements of forgetfulness, mistakenness, embellishment, exaggeration? Difficult to say.

The detectives battled on through November into December, obtaining dust sample after sample, taking statements, patrolling the streets and the lonely places where the prostitutes took their clients and talking, talking to anyone who could provide anything, even a modicum of intelligence to provide a clue to the killer; but nobody did.

Christmas came and went and on Boxing Day, Manchester Police commenced a missing person enquiry after ten-year-old Lesley Ann Downey went missing from a fairground in Ancoats. Although Manchester police were unaware of the connection, six months earlier they had commenced another missing person enquiry, that of 12- year-old Keith Bennett, who had disappeared at Fallowfield. It would take another ten months for Ian Brady and Myra Hindley to be arrested for their murders – together with the murders of three other children, at least four of whom had been sexually assaulted. Depraved serial killers were certainly not confined to London.

Back in London, the weather in January 1965 was fairly cold with some sunshine but frosty nights. February was cold and it was halfway through that month that the next body was found.

VICTIM NO. 8

BRIDGET O'HARA

The Surgical Equipment Supplies Ltd was one of the many factories on the Heron Trading Estate, Acton, W3. One of its employees was Leonard Ernest Beauchamp and at about 10.30 on the morning of Tuesday, 16 February 1965, he had occasion to go to one of his company's store sheds. When he looked behind the main store shed, he saw two feet protruding from the undergrowth. It was difficult for Beauchamp to ascertain exactly what it was he'd found; it could have been a tailor's dummy. The reason for the difficulty was because between the sheds and a chain link fence was a passageway, about 2ft 6in wide. This was filled with undergrowth, some 2ft high; it was also used as a dumping ground for miscellaneous rubbish.

So if the discovery of something resembling a body was causing Beauchamp some difficulty as to what it actually was, it proved even more difficult to convince his workmates. Eventually, the company's production manager, Gerald Humphreys West Marshall, took a look for himself, and since tailors' dummies do not usually have painted toenails, he was satisfied it was a human body and called the police.

Some fibres were found in the close vicinity and these might have come from Messrs Beauchamp or Marshall, but fortunately neither of them had interfered with the body. However, somebody had; dried and dead grass had been torn up from the adjoining ground in an effort to conceal the body.

Within half an hour of the discovery of the body, the police had arrived in force; Baldock was accompanied by DI Crabb plus two liaison officers from the Metropolitan Police Scientific Laboratory: DCI Napier and DS Trapp; with them was the principal scientific officer, Thomas Jones. From the Yard's fingerprint department came DCS Godsell and Det. Supt Robertson and the photographic branch was represented by senior photographer McLean. The pathologist, Dr David Bowen, was at St George's Hospital, Hyde Park Corner, when he received a telephone call; it took him very little time to get to the scene. Also present was the coroner, Dr Harold Broadbridge, and to officially pronounce life extinct, the Divisional Surgeon, Dr M. Morgan.

That was the easy part; the naked body of Bridget Esther O'Hara, alias Bridie Moore, certainly was dead and that was Dr Morgan's small, but important part in the investigation completed. He was now free to insert an entry in Acton police station's Book 83 to claim his recompense for being dragged out of his surgery at the unholy hour of 11 o'clock in the morning.

O'Hara's dental plate was missing and, like all of the other victims, she was a prostitute, she had been asphyxiated and stripped after death. And again, there was the telltale spotting of paint on her body.

Before removal to the mortuary, Dr Bowen gave the body a cursory examination. It had all the appearances of being well preserved. There was some generalised pallor but no obvious injuries. He noted there was some slight sogginess of the skin on her back and this suggested that where the body had lain, it had been there only for a short time. There were various opinions regarding this; however, everyone agreed it could not have been there for more than fourteen days. That was all, for the time being. Forty forensic specimens were obtained from the scene for onward transmission to the police laboratory.

Meanwhile, Baldock was, in police parlance, 'giving his eyes a treat'. Where the body had been hidden was approximately 108ft from the Westfields Road, which led in turn on to Alliance Road, a thoroughfare right through the estate and into the Western Avenue. Only by crossing the bridge over the LTE Central London railway line connecting West Acton with North Acton could access be made to the estate. Next, the chain link fence next to where the body had been found formed the boundary of the estate. It separated the steep railway embankments that dipped down

25ft between the estate and the rear gardens of the houses on Highfield Road, a distance of 275ft, and therefore the visual distance would make it difficult for anyone overlooking the area to observe anything that would be of assistance; in daylight hours, that is. At night-time it was thought to be impossible but, impossible or not, this had to be checked and it was. As expected, nobody saw anything.

But it proved one thing. The murderer certainly knew his way around the area; and when he dumped O'Hara's body, he was tolerably certain that he would not be observed – and he wasn't.

So with the body en route to the mortuary, measurements being carried out, photographs taken, the shaken Mr Beauchamp making a statement and all the hundred-and-one other things that accompany the onset of a murder enquiry, Bill Baldock assumed control of the investigation. Why not? After all, the body had been found on 'T' Division, and he was the head of the CID for that area of the Metropolitan Police.

However, it was an appointment that would not last for long.

★★★

Before we turn to the rather extraordinary turn of events that occurred next (and I'm referring to the supremacy aspect of the investigation, rather than anything else), the antecedents of Bridget O'Hara, who was born Bridget Esther Moore in Dublin in 1937, should be mentioned.

They are depressing enough. The sixth of twelve children, she attended school in Dublin until the age of 14, from when she worked as a factory hand and a hospital domestic until 1955, when she came to London and was similarly employed. In 1956 she collected her first conviction for soliciting prostitution; in the two years that followed she gathered ten more. She was last arrested for this offence on 14 May 1958 and upon being bailed to attend Marylebone Magistrates' Court, she failed to appear. Although a warrant was issued for her arrest, it was never executed and, in fact, was withdrawn on 2 August 1963.

However, later enquiries revealed she continued soliciting in the Bayswater, Notting Hill, Holland Park and Shepherd's Bush districts, and was picked up by punters in their cars and also in cafés and pubs. As far as could be ascertained, she never brought punters back to any of her own addresses but was known to go to the homes of her clients. She exaggerated her conquests, telling her associates of her 'sugar daddies' – one such philanthropic character, a 53-year-old businessman, was traced, interviewed and quickly eliminated from the enquiry – but, as Baldock would later assert, '… her sexual aberrations knew no bounds providing there was, by her standards, sufficient financial remuneration. This would generally amount to no more than £2 or £3.'

Had he known of Baldock's comments, John Newman would have agreed with them. 'She was a part-time girl who sold herself to pay the rent or for food,' he told me; this was confirmed by the fact she would obtain casual, but legitimate employment, albeit for brief periods.

She had moved in with 24-year-old Michael O'Hara upon her arrival in London in 1955; he had first come to the notice of police four years earlier than Moore. He had eleven convictions for serious crime, including shopbreaking, assault, importuning and larceny, and after being released from an eighteen-month sentence on 13 December 1961, he and Moore were married in September 1962. Although it would be a childless liaison, it appeared that Bridget O'Hara did want a family; she had suffered a miscarriage at home in March 1962 and fertility tests carried out at the antenatal clinic at Hammersmith Hospital on 1 May 1964 revealed she was physically capable of bearing children.

Desirous of raising a family or not, it was a miserable marriage, full of drunkenness, fights and crockery being thrown. Their last address, one furnished room in a top-floor flat with communal washing and cooking facilities at 41 Agate Road, Hammersmith, was adroitly turned into a pigsty. It was little wonder that none of her 'sugar daddies' were invited back there and also confirms the doubts that existed as to their beneficence.

An alcoholic with a vicious temper, O'Hara was obstreperous and violent in drink; when anybody crossed her, even during her periods of sobriety, she would make her objections known forcibly, both verbally and physically. She and her husband (who would later unconvincingly tell police he had finally persuaded her to give up her life of prostitution) were known to frequent almost every public house that attracted 'a low -class clientele' in the Hammersmith, Notting Hill and Shepherd's Bush districts.

Three days prior to the evening of 11 January 1965 (which was the last time Bridget O'Hara was seen alive), the O'Haras had made a concerted effort to repair their domestic difficulties and had started to live what, for them, was a normal married life. Michael O'Hara had commenced working on a building site at London Heathrow Airport. On 11 January he returned home at 6.30 p.m., and they both consumed a casserole she had prepared. In fact, the autopsy would confirm her stomach contents were consistent with having eaten such a meal and this would assist in determining the time of her death.

According to her husband, they had only 11s between them and therefore at 9.30 p.m., Bridget O'Hara left in order to borrow some money from her friend, Mrs Jean Mary Havelock.

She was smartly dressed for the occasion: a three button, loose-fitting grey tweed coat with a herringbone pattern – attached to the coat was a scarf of the same material with a black fringe – a fawn cardigan, a red and black mottled pattern blouse and a black skirt.

To get to Mrs Havelock's address she would have had to walk a fairly short distance from her flat, crossing Shepherd's Bush Road. Whether she changed her mind (or had no intention of going there), she did not arrive at Mrs Havelock's home. Instead, she walked along Goldhawk Road and arrived at the Shepherd's Bush Hotel at Shepherd's Bush Green. There she was seen by two Irish brothers, Edward and Joseph Kelly, at approximately 10.20 p.m.. The brothers saw her speak to a man, later identified as William John Kelly – known as Jock (no relation to the brothers and not to be confused with the late security guard, of whom, more later) – and she had a drink with him. She later came over to the brothers' table and chatted with them, referring to Jock as being 'just a friend'. Edward Kelly left the bar at 11.15 p.m. and did not see Bridget O'Hara thereafter; Joseph Kelly stated that he left the pub shortly after his brother and saw Bridget O'Hara and Jock Kelly leave and walk off together.

Having made that statement to police, Edward Kelly met Jock, again at the Shepherd's Bush Hotel and he told him he had not left with Bridget; she had left with another man, also a Scot, and that he had heard that this man, following an argument with a woman either in Acton or Chiswick, had attempted to strangle her.

Jock was traced and provided three statements in which he more or less concurred with the accounts given by the Kelly brothers and stated that he had first met Bridget on the run-up to Christmas week in 1964 at the Shepherd's Bush Hotel. She had been in the company of another woman, 'Flo', and two Welshmen who were believed to be brothers; also another man aged about 40. This was the man, said Jock, whom he had seen walk off with Bridget; he described him as being 5ft 6in tall, heavy build, full face, fresh complexion with dark brown hair. He had been wearing a dark brown suede three-quarter length jacket with a fleecy collar, a green or brown trilby hat and greyish trousers. He denied saying to Edward Kelly that the man was a Scot and although he agreed he had said this man had attempted to strangle a woman, this was only gossip.

'Flo' was identified as Mrs Flora Forbes, a 31-year-old barmaid, and she agreed with Jock's account of the pre-Christmas meeting. Upon leaving the pub at 11 p.m. that night, Mrs Forbes told police that she, Bridget and their three companions – the two Welsh brothers and the other man – went to Coco's Club, Shepherd's Bush Green, where they danced until two o'clock the following morning; whereupon Bridget walked off with the third, older man.

Mrs Forbes could not assist regarding the identities of the brothers or the other man; she provided a description of him that vaguely agreed with Jock's portrayal of the man and although a description of this man was circulated to the press on the day following Jock Kelly's final statement, and despite the most searching enquires that were carried out to trace them, none of the three men have ever been identified. An identikit picture of the third man was assembled but it was of such poor quality that it was considered it would possibly lead to confusion and therefore it was never circulated.

Whomever it was that Bridget O'Hara left the Shepherd's Bush Hotel with late on the evening of 11 January it appears she did so quite happily, arm in arm; her to oblivion, him to goodness-knows-where.

★★★

After making fruitless enquiries as to his wife's whereabouts from her associates, on 3 February 1965, Michael O'Hara reported her disappearance to Hammersmith police station. She was not treated as a missing person as such – a 'Misper' in police parlance – because she, like many prostitutes, had previously gone missing voluntarily, so her details were duly noted in the station's Occurrence Book, that thick dun-coloured tome, measuring 15in × 10in, which was kept in the front office of every police station. No circulation to other stations was considered necessary; it was noted that she had left her husband previously ('to cohabit with other men, having little regard for the type of person she lived with' commented Baldock) and had returned.

It makes for uncomfortable reading to know that at the time her disappearance was reported to police, Bridget O'Hara's body was in the possession of her murderer and there it remained, almost certainly until 6 o'clock on the morning of 12 February.

It was then that Mrs Thelma Schwartz, a 28-year-old cleaner, was on her way to work at the Zonal Films Facilities Ltd on the Heron Trading Estate and as she passed the unmade road (where the body was found) she heard the sound of rustling and movements some 35 yards away; she described them as distinct, unusual and, for the time of the night, very loud. She became so frightened that she ran the 400 yards to her place of work; and fortunately the person making the noises could not have heard her because Mrs Schwarz was wearing rubber-soled shoes.

She mentioned the incident to her mother and when the body was discovered, four days later, it was again the nature of excited comment to her mother and neighbours.

It was as a result of 'not wanting to get involved' that not until over three months later, on 19 May, and through a great deal of persistence from one of the officers on this enquiry, a DS Colligan from 'V' Division, that this information was revealed. Thousands of people on the estate had been questioned and countless enquiries, publicity and appeals had been made, yet it beggars belief that nobody who was aware of this vital piece of information had come forward.

Seven months previously, with the discovery of Mary Fleming's body, the American press had decided upon a suitable *nom de guerre* for the murderer: 'Jack the Stripper' and this was adopted by the British newspapers, knowing a catchy nickname when they saw one. Although the investigators of all the other murders had been working as hard as they could with their limited resources, the Yard decided they must be seen to be doing more. They, too needed a nickname to rely upon and to strengthen public confidence. In consequence, they brought out their ace of trumps: 'Four Day Johnny'.

ENTER JOHN DU ROSE

John Valentine Ralph Du Rose once told a colleague, 'Investigation is useless, unless it is followed through with absolute persistence from the very beginning.' It was probably the failure to convict anyone for the murder of Countess Teresa Lubienska in 1957, when 18,000 statements were taken and where the investigation dragged on for years, that led him to make that statement. It changed Du Rose's whole concept of murder investigation – and he was already a successful murder investigator – so that thereafter he would marshal a massive strike force of officers to act in such cases; and it was a technique that had worked.

Du Rose had been born in 1911 in Lambeth. One of seven children, he was just 9 when his father died of wounds he had received in the First World War. There was, of course, no question of any further education and he left school as soon as possible to become the family breadwinner.

Relinquishing his job as a furniture salesman and joining the Metropolitan Police as Police Constable 254 'C' in 1931, he patrolled the streets of Soho and very quickly developed the knack of being able to spot lawbreakers instinctively. One such case led to him being commended by the magistrate at Marlborough Street Police Court and when car batteries were being stolen regularly from a yard, he followed the trail of battery acid, sometimes on his hands and knees, until it led him to the receiver's yard and the recovery of all the stolen property. This and other smart arrests prompted him to apply to be an aid to CID and in the eighteen months that followed, he and his partner carried out 180 arrests.

He was in good company. Within months of Du Rose joining the police, tall, wiry Matthew Brinnand also arrived at 'C' Division. Brinnand went on to become a leading light on the Flying Squad and was one of the original four members of the highly secretive post-war Ghost Squad, due to the number of informants he had acquired in London's West End. They provided him with information for the simple reason they were too frightened of him to do anything else. And the detective inspector (second class) was Peter Beveridge, the red-haired Scot who had been wounded during active service with the Seaforth Highlanders in the First World War; a martinet but a first-rate detective, Beveridge (who would go on to head the war-time Flying Squad) was an inspiration to his men.

These were the type of men from whom Du Rose learnt his trade as a detective, inside and out; he was a constable and sergeant for twenty-three years, and then in the following fifteen years his career rocketed, rising to the rank of deputy assistant commissioner.

He was a thorough, plodding detective rather than a dashing one; as a detective sergeant (second class) at Bow Street police station, he complained that it was difficult to obtain information from the Covent Garden market fraternity, although this was nonsense. Jack Capstick had a myriad of informants from that section of society; however, as a constable on the beat, he had become involved in fights with several of the porters who cheeked him and it was probably the admiration that they held for Capstick (for bashing, rather than arresting them) that promoted them to take him into their confidence.

As a young police officer, Du Rose had been a great worrier; could he have done more to detect a case – or having brought a case to court, had he done everything possible to make sure it was absolutely watertight?

Age, rank and experience gave him more confidence. In the years that followed, legends began to grow about Du Rose; it was said he was responsible for the arrest of the serial murderer, John George Haigh, who dissolved his victims in acid. In fact, following the disappearance of one of his victims, Du Rose interviewed Haigh, disbelieved his story and reported the matter to his senior officers – that was all. He was credited with smashing up the

Messina brothers' vice empire; but that enquiry was started by Det. Supt Guy Mahon in 1951 and it was not until 1958 that Du Rose appeared on the scene. He arrested one of the brothers, Carmelo, for possessing a false passport but that was only as the result of a talented woman detective sergeant's informant pointing them in the right direction; and the same woman sergeant's information brought about the arrest and conviction of brother Attilio the following year. It did Du Rose no harm at all, especially since by now, Guy Mahon was eighteen months into his retirement and with no one to share the plaudits, three months later, it secured Du Rose's promotion to detective superintendent.

This is not meant to diminish Du Rose's successes in any way; he did have a number of spectacular successes that resulted in Owen Summers, a *Daily Mail* reporter dubbing him Four Day Johnny because of the speed in which he solved murder cases. Matters became a little scrambled when he was also referred to as Three Day Johnny and also One Day Johnny – perhaps the one-day murderers gave themselves up, having already penned a full confession to save time. And as his fame grew, so his career was splattered with commendations: he was praised for his ability in a case of demanding money with menaces, as was his persistence in a case of robbery. Both his 'ability and persistence' was lauded in cases of arson and also in effecting the arrest of a housebreaker who, it appeared, was every bit as persistent as the arresting officer. He provided 'initiative and ability' in a difficult case of blackmail and in cases of both murder and manslaughter he lent the enquiries his 'valuable assistance'. Fraudsters who committed offences of false pretences and fraudulent conversion were added to the list, as were warehousebreakers, shopbreakers, receivers and larcenists.

By 1 August 1963, DCS Du Rose was one of The Big Five, the head of C1 Department at the Yard; it was he who now tasked the detectives to investigate murders, at home and abroad. As well as murders, C1 Department also dealt with forgery, drugs, false passports, illegal immigrants, government liaison and also industrial espionage. One such case of sabotage was dealt with by the then DC (and later DCI) David Pritchard, who arrested the man responsible. The man pleaded guilty and was committed to the Quarter Sessions for sentence. The Director of Public Prosecutions (who had instigated the enquiry) was delighted and Du Rose was furious; Pritchard had breached the rules by taking an official into his confidence in order to identify, arrest and induce the culprit to confess. Despite Pritchard stating that unless he had acted decisively the man could have carried out his threat to cause explosions at the Royal Marine (Reserve) Building and the Inland Revenue, resulting in a great deal of damage to government property, together with a possible loss of life, Du Rose castigated the young detective. However, it was at variance with the remarks he made to a colleague when he said, 'There is a tendency, an awful tendency for officers to abide by the rules entirely. An officer today can't be a stick-in-the-mud. I believe in rules but not in interpreting them as narrowly as possible.' It also smacked of double standards; whereas I like to think that someone like Baldock, more concerned with the practicalities of the matter, would have roared with laughter at Pritchard's ingenuity and poured him a large Scotch.

Du Rose was well respected but not necessarily liked; the late Arthur Phillips (who had featured in the Figg investigation) told me, 'His favourite expression was, "Not that, Matey – not that",' adding, 'it was said to make you feel small.'

In less than three months, Du Rose would be propelled out of his office armchair; he was directed to make enquiries into the activities of one DS Harold Gordon Challenor MM of West End Central police station. Challenor (together with three aids to CID) was accused of planting house bricks on members of the public during a very noisy demonstration, protesting about Queen Fredericka of Greece, during a state visit.

Anarchists who took part in the demonstration assumed the enquiry would be a whitewash, as did the National Council for Civil Liberties who supported them; it was nothing of the kind. Du Rose took nothing at face value and carried out a deep-searching investigation. Following the arrest of Challenor and the aids, Challenor was diagnosed as being a paranoid schizophrenic and unfit to stand trial; he was committed to a psychiatric hospital where he remained for three years. The aids were sentenced to long periods of imprisonment. The public enquiry that followed commenced on 28 September 1964 and concluded two months later, having examined and cross-examined 132 witnesses. It had taken a year out of Du Rose's life and he was exhausted. He and his wife, Constance, were looking forward to a much needed holiday, which started and finished on 16 February 1965.

The couple had just arrived at the holiday bungalow at St Mary's Bay, Kent, when a sergeant from the local Dymchurch police station knocked on the door to ask him to telephone the Yard. He did so and discovered that the Assistant Commissioner (Crime) demanded his presence back in London to take overall charge of the murdered prostitutes enquiry.

★★★

Du Rose's arrival on the squad was greeted in *The Evening News*, dated 17 February 1965, with the headlines, 'The Trap to Catch a Killer' together with the murderer's identikit picture superimposed over a map of London with, as a sub-heading, 'Expert is Recalled'. All would be well, now that Four Day Johnny was on the case. The *Chicago Tribune* certainly thought so. With its banner headline of 18 February, it proclaimed, 'Scotland Yard searches for slayer of 7 prostitutes' with 'London combed for man with round face' as a sub-heading. Its readers were informed – slightly inaccurately – 'Detective Superintendent John Du Rose, who has never failed to solve a murder case, was called back from vacation to take charge of the investigation'. And according to 'a police source', it was suggested that 'The man may be a hen-pecked husband taking vicarious revenge or a morality maniac'.

'Whilst I'm sure Bill Baldock wasn't pleased at being replaced by John Du Rose,' John Newman told me, 'I can assure you that it was Du Rose who was incandescent at times about having his holiday cancelled and being put in charge of the squad.'

Newman was right on both counts; Du Rose was furious at having his well-deserved holiday cancelled, as was Baldock at being, as he saw it, usurped. Although they had never worked together before, Baldock was not a big admirer of Du Rose; his lip tended to curl whenever Owen Summers' nickname of Four Day Johnny was mentioned and he felt he could have overseen the enquiry by himself. After all, he had conducted the Barthelemy enquiry and had undoubtedly learned much regarding the aspects of the other murders from his fellow investigating officers.

However, great detective though he was, Baldock's investigative skills as a murder investigator were limited, whereas Du Rose had spent three tours of his career at C1 Department and he had a long series of successes catching killers. Most important of all, Baldock did not possess a nickname known to the public – and to restore confidence the Yard needed to send out a Four Day Johnny so the investigation could be resolved in double-quick time. (Frank Davies did have a nickname; due to his unfortunate choice of footwear he was referred to as 'Jeepers' after the type of shoes worn by Teddy Boys that were known as Brothel Creepers. There was also a popular 1938 song by Harry Warren and Johnny Mercer, *Jeepers Creepers*, and he was furious when he made his entrance at an annual Flying Squad dinner and dance and the whole audience burst into a chorus of that particular melody. But not only had Davies charged an innocent man with the murder of Irene Lockwood, Jeepers was not a nickname which would inspire public confidence – Four Day Johnny was.)

'Du Rose and Baldock were two completely different characters,' Bob Cook remembered. 'Bill Baldock, suave, relaxed and friendly, usually with a big lardy (cigar) on the go, Du Rose somewhat serious and a bit dour.' And Terry Babbidge recalled that Du Rose, 'was more like a military man – a good Guv'nor,' adding that Baldock, too was, 'a very good Guv'nor.'

An incident room was set up at Shepherd's Bush police station and all the statements and exhibits from the other murder investigations were brought there, together with the indices. There was absolutely no doubt that at least six of the murders were linked (with the possibility of Elizabeth Figg as well; Rees had more or less been eliminated as a non-starter) and almost certainly carried out by the same man, therefore the index cards were intermingled.

To familiarise himself with the murders, Du Rose started ploughing through all the statements; to assist him, he had DI Kenneth Gordon Oxford, whom he had brought with him from the Yard. Oxford was now 41. Joining the police after wartime service with RAF Bomber Command, he had assisted in the controversial A6 murder enquiry that had had resulted in James Hanratty being hanged. It was he who arrested Christine Keeler for perjury and latterly he had assisted Du Rose in the Challenor investigation. 'Sometimes blunt, but honest and direct,' were Bryan Martin's comments.

To assist Baldock, he had the services of DI Edward Albert Crabb. This former schoolteacher had returned to the police after seeing war service as a captain in the Middlesex Regiment and in 1948 was awarded a commissioner's commendation for 'great courage and determination in dealing with a large gang of armed criminals' – this referred to the fight that resulted in heavy casualties on both sides, which the press dubbed 'The Battle of Heathrow'.[*]

So Du Rose, scowling at his holiday mistreatment, puffing on his inevitable cheroots, his thickset body inclined over a mound of statements, his leonine head nodding as he noted important issues, got to work – and suddenly, two days after his arrival, it appeared that his nickname was justified because it looked as though an astonishing breakthrough in the investigation had been made.

---

[*] For further information regarding this thrilling chapter in the Flying Squad's history, see *The Sweeney: The First Sixty Years of Scotland Yard's Crimebusting Flying Squad 1919–1978*, Pen & Sword Books, 2011.

DU ROSE'S INVESTIGATION

This aspect of the enquiry had actually commenced some two months earlier, when a prostitute was interviewed on 9 December 1964 during the Frances Brown murder investigation. She told police of her sexual experiences with three men in a garage in Hammersmith, the previous night; they were the proprietor (referred to here as 'White'), a mechanic (referred to here as 'Brown') and a car dealer (referred to here as 'Green').

The three men were interviewed and they admitted the various sexual acts as the prostitute had described; no offences of a sexual nature were disclosed. This aspect of the enquiry was not considered to be particularly pressing and therefore, due to the sheer volume of the work, it was not until 12 February 1965 that the garage was visited by DS Bob Berry, who took dust and paint samples from the garage door that he later handed to Thomas Jones, one of the scientific officers at the police laboratory, for analysis.

But on 18 February, two days after the discovery of O'Hara's body, an urgent conference was called by the forensic staff at the laboratory. Although the examination of the samples of debris that had been taken from the garage was not complete, the sample was found optically to be similar to dust and paint samples found on the bodies of four of the murdered women. In fact, stated Mr Jones, none of the many previous samples had displayed such striking similarities.

The very same day, the garage was swamped by Mr Jones, lab liaison officers, fingerprint officers, officers from Scotland Yard's Stolen Vehicle Squad and the photographic section, and the three men were brought to the station to be interviewed, in all probability in circumstances less genial than before.

All of them made lengthy statements – White's alone came to thirteen pages – and their home addresses were searched, White's house by Bryan Martin, who had accompanied DIs Ted Crabb and Ken Oxford. 'Ted insisted we took out the fireplace surround and the hollow walls,' Martin told me. Nothing incriminating was found in any of the three addresses and while two of the men were released, the garage owner, 'White', was detained overnight. Meanwhile, the inquest into O'Hara's death was held in which the pathologist stated that death had been due to asphyxia after pressure on the face and neck had been applied, and the hearing was adjourned until 17 March.

The following day a Luger pistol and ammunition were found in the garage's roof space. There was a ridiculous allegation made that the items had been planted by police to permit them more time to question White. Nothing could have been further from the truth; no further progress had been made, the line of questioning had been exhausted and the garage owner was about to be released when the items were discovered. They were shown to White, who disclaimed any knowledge of them but did agree that only he possessed keys to the garage. He was charged with receiving the items and also not having a firearms certificate. Appearing at court the next day, he was remanded in custody until 26 February, when the receiving charge was dismissed. At a further appearance, the remaining charge was also dismissed and he was awarded twenty guineas from public funds. There had been enormous press publicity following the man's appearance in court. As the officer obtaining the preliminary remand, DI Crabb was asked if the 'further enquires' he had mentioned were anything to do with a murder enquiry; he replied blandly, 'I cannot answer that question.'

Meanwhile, it was necessary to speak to a man, who will be referred to here as 'Black', also a car dealer, said to have been in possession of two guns, who also frequented that garage. It appeared he had made himself unavailable to the police deliberately and on the evening of 20 February 1965 an appeal was launched on both television and through the press to trace him since no one, it seemed, had any idea as to his whereabouts. No one that is except 'White's' solicitor, who produced 'Black' at Shepherd's Bush police station the very next day. 'Black' refused to make a statement but during his two-hour stay reluctantly answered the questions put to him. At the time of one of the murders he was able to prove that he was in custody at Brixton prison, awaiting trial for officebreaking. It had been a tempest in a teacup that could easily have been avoided and resulted in a great deal of unnecessary publicity.

Writs were served on the police by the garage owner's solicitor alleging malicious prosecution and false imprisonment but this, as Baldock commented contemptuously, was 'purely as a means of obtaining money from the police'. He did; 'White' accepted £1,000 as an out of court settlement.

To be fair, this was the strongest lead the police had got. Although the car dealer 'Green' had been one of the two men released initially, his replies in response to the questions put to him had been most vague and reticent. Furthermore, it was discovered he visited the same pubs in the Shepherd's Bush Green area as both the O'Haras and that he associated with prostitutes from that vicinity. More than anything else, he had a slight resemblance to the man who had been seen to leave with O'Hara and who was shown in the identikit picture compiled by William John Kelly and Flora Forbes. That being so, he was put up for identification on the morning of 21 February 1965 at Shepherd's Bush police station; Kelly attended the parade but no identification was made.

Three men had encountered a prostitute in a garage where paint had been discovered very similar to that found on the bodies of four of the dead prostitutes – and there was more.

During the same month that Brown was murdered, she had told a friend of a rather frightening encounter she had on the previous evening when a man in a small van – believed to be grey – had stopped her and produced a small black card with 'Metropolitan Police' in gold lettering. This, of course, was what a police warrant card looked like at that time and the man told her that he 'was CID'. They had discussed the murdered prostitutes and he had said the murderer had pulled their outer clothing down over their arms, trapping them; this was a common ploy used in a roughhouse. He then said that the clothing that the victims were wearing underneath was twisted round their necks, and this had the ring of plausibility about it. Brown was quite disturbed with the way that the conversation was going and left. She had noted there was some clothing in the back of the van but she had not provided a description of the man to her friend.

Going on from there, when the prostitute volunteered the information to the police about the three occupants of the garage, she said the garage owner, 'White', introduced himself initially as Bert Roberts and said he was a CID officer from Scotland Yard. She suggested that he resembled the identikit picture of the man who had driven off with Kim Taylor.

She also mentioned that the car dealer, 'Green', looked like the picture of the man who had gone with Frances Brown. The men had conveyed the prostitute to the garage in a cream van and yet, if the van existed, it appeared that it was not examined forensically and neither of the men were put up for identification by Kim Taylor.

Taking all that into account, there must be a link. There had to be. But the alibis of the men's whereabouts on the nights of the murders stood up; and there wasn't.

★★★

Baldock was experiencing the greatest difficulties with his enquiries into the O'Hara family due to their mode of life and their associates, the majority of whom had criminal records or were living just outside the law. Although these persons were deeply shocked that one of their own had met a violent end, there had been a constant fear, by reason of their own misdeeds, of involvement in an enquiry such as this.

As Baldock would later say:

> The statements obtained have revealed lies and counter-lies selfishly cover-ing their own petty nefarious and sexual activities, stubbornly refusing to appreciate the main object of our investigations – to find the killer. Such is their mentality and the pattern of their lives that their days and weeks are one, revolving around a little work, an excess of alcohol, sex and sleep, so that even if they desired to tell the truth, little or no reliance could be placed on their memory of dates or events.

The victim's husband, Michael O'Hara, came in for special criticism, with Baldock describing him as:

> … an indolent individual; an apt composite of all that one can find objectionable in the introduction to this particular investigation. His assistance in this enquiry has been almost useless. Invariably, when interviewed he was drunk, which rendered any observations unreliable. Even when kept at the station until sober, his condition was such that he was incapable of giving a coherent story. Only when interrogated most firmly has anything like the truth been elicited.

(This last sentence is, of course, open to reasonably wide interpretation.)

★★★

Du Rose now set his 'strike force' plan in motion. According to Baldock, 'the pathetically few men available' commenced night-duty patrols on 19 February, on foot, with the telephone being their only means of communication. Four days later, authorisation was granted for twenty-eight officers to use their private cars to patrol an area of 24 square miles covering the whole of 'F' Division and parts of 'T', 'V' and 'X' Divisions. Duke's Meadows was patrolled in particular, as were car parks, cul-de-sacs, railway arches and open and secluded places where prostitutes took their clients. So was the area from Hammersmith Bridge to Chiswick Bridge where the bodies of Tailford and Lockwood had been found; this area of the Thames was the subject of special attention by the night-duty patrols of the River Police.

On 26 February, a young woman who had been spotted by a woman police officer as bearing a striking similarity to Bridget O'Hara was induced to parade in clothing identical to that worn by O'Hara on the last time she was seen, outside Shepherd's Bush police station. The photograph was circulated in a Special Notice in *Police Gazette*, dated 1 March 1965. Television crews filmed her and press photographers snapped her. This was given the maximum publicity to see if anyone could recall seeing O'Hara since her disappearance, but nobody did. In addition, press conferences were held twice daily, morning and evening, at Shepherd's Bush police station. From time to time, photographs of the dead women were shown, as was clothing and jewellery similar to that worn by them.

The night-duty squad was augmented on 9 March – and not before time – to comprise six CID officers, fifty-eight aids to CID, four women officers and eight male officers, all in plain clothes, who were under the supervision of a detective inspector.

One of the constables in plain clothes was Keith Buxton and he was transported to a fixed point; in his case a 'Tardis-style' police box situated on the approach to Chertsey Bridge from Chiswick. 'My job was to sit inside this "Tardis" with my pad of pro formas clocking all the vehicles in and out,' he told me. 'These pro formas were taken to the vehicle registration office in central London for checking. From time to time, they would send me a note if anything of interest arose; celebrities such as showbiz stars, sportspeople and, of course, MPs and peers of the realm were fairly common.' Bob Hayday, then an aid to CID, was also made privy to some of the names. 'Nothing changes, does it!' was his comment to me.

Another police box was used as a fixed point; this one was situated opposite Wormwood Scrubs Prison and on occasion it was manned by Malcolm Peacock, an aid from 'G' Division. 'Strangely enough, no one gave it a second glance as they passed,' he told me. 'It was just daylight when two burglars crossed the road in front of the box, broke into the school opposite and were very surprised to be caught by the RT crew who'd been summoned by me using the box telephone!'

One of the many aids was Geoff Cameron who, with his partner (or 'buck'), Ken Graham, had been seconded from 'S' Division. He told me:

When we arrived, we were taken aback by the size of the enquiry, manpower-wise. I reckon my buck and I were just two amongst some sixty aids to CID. I don't know the strength of the daytime squad, but there were many. I could count on three fingers the times I saw Du Rose. We were controlled at night by local DCs and a DS from 'F' Division who gave us our briefing and that was it. For the aids, it was not a good enquiry to be on and quite honestly, I and many others were glad when our time was run. One thing the 'Jack the Stripper' murders taught me later in my service was the necessity to communicate with the troops and not to leave them in the dark.

Rod Bellis agreed with those sentiments. 'When we first met, we were briefed by John Du Rose and possibly, Bill Baldock,' he told me, adding, 'we never saw them again.' However, that point was taken up by John Newman who, as a detective constable was sometimes employed driving Du Rose to his home at Daybrook Road, Merton Park, SW19. 'I found him pleasant company and interested in knowing what the morale and feelings of those employed on "nights" were,' he told me. 'As we – those on nights – had no idea what was happening during the daytime and what, if any use was being made of the details of the lone drivers we were supplying, I said that it would help if we knew those details. The next night when we reported for duty, he spoke with us all, detailing the work of checking the car numbers, owners, addresses and the interviews.'

Keith Buxton, too, remembered Du Rose: 'He would visit us nights, to bring us up to date. I can see him now, all these years later. A big man in a double-breasted grey suit; his nickname – Four Day Johnny.'

Whether those seconded to the enquiry felt it was productive or onerous, Du Rose insisted that it be declared a 'special occasion'. This meant that instead of receiving the niggardly detective duty allowance that was paid monthly to CID officers, irrespective of the number of hours worked, all the officers were paid overtime on a parity with uniform officers. It meant that their wages doubled plus, with expenses and mileage allowance, they sometimes trebled.

The Special Patrol Group had just been formed; Du Rose applied to the Assistant Commissioner 'A' Department, John Waldron (later Commissioner Sir John Waldron, KCVO) for their assistance and for the first three weeks following the squad's inception, the enquiry team's numbers were further increased by 300 officers.

As well as the initial lack of officers, the biggest problem was communications. A transmitting set was installed at Shepherd's Bush police station by 'D' Department. It needed a great deal of experimentation by the District Communications Officer from No. 1 District and in view of the large area to be covered, three radio vans with wireless operators were positioned at strategic points in the area. A special channel was allocated and the officers were issued with what were then referred to as 'walkie-talkie' sets to communicate with the base. Since 1946, the Cossor Company had been providing the police with portable radio transmitters and communications would be substantially improved in 1969 with the introduction of Stornophone VHF equipment. However, in 1965, the police had to use whatever they could get; Bob Cook recalled that they were 'big and crude'. Rod Bellis described them as being 'large, like a telephone'. Bryan Martin spent some time in the communications room. 'One example of the primitive set-up was that one night the radio messages we were getting were very clear but confusing,' he told me. 'We eventually found that the unusual air conditions meant that a radio message from a force in the Midlands was coming through on our frequency.'

All the registration numbers of vehicles seen after midnight on major and side roads and secluded spots were noted, together with the date, time, place and if possible a description of the occupant, noted on specially designed pro forma.

It was emphasised to the officers that practically any type of vehicle could be used by the murderer to convey the victim: car, van, cab, estate or commercial vehicle, including those bearing trade plates. In fact, any type of vehicle capable of carrying a body, particularly one that contained only one occupant or a man and a woman. This particularly applied to many British Airways coaches since they were frequent in the area as they ferried passengers to Heathrow Airport, all night. 'Ted Crabb complained about this,' said Rod Bellis, 'but eventually conceded that as some of the coaches only had the driver on board, they couldn't be ruled out.'

If a vehicle was seen more than once, the details were recorded separately and in this way, the particular route of a vehicle, sometimes circling an area several times could be followed. Therefore, it followed that officers seeing any vehicle under any circumstances that they considered to be suspicious were specially noted.

Peter Westacott was a detective constable at Gerald Road police station who had been seconded on to the night-duty squad and while patrolling with his partner, David Heath, they spotted a vehicle – perhaps displaying a part-registration plate – which was of interest to the enquiry. They detained the driver, brought him into the police station and Du Rose was called. Westacott was worried that the great man might take umbrage at being called from his bed in the middle of the night; he need not have worried.

'He listened carefully to everything I had to say,' Westacott told me, 'and then invited me and my partner to be present during the suspect's interview.' In fact, the man had nothing to do with the murders and was soon released but Westacott was deeply impressed that Du Rose had taken the trouble to include him in that aspect of the enquiry. 'He was a good guy,' recalled Westacott, 'always said "hello" and treated us well.'

The majority of the officers employed on these night-duty observations were allocated a 'beat' and these were slightly overlapped so that constant coverage was maintained. In addition to these beats, specific observation points were set up at Notting Hill, Kensington and Shepherd's Bush, the known areas where prostitutes operated, and special attention was paid to punters or kerb-crawlers. Mike Nadin was an aid to CID at Chelsea and he and his partner were part of the night-duty patrols. 'We worked 6 p.m. to 6 a.m. continuously, driving our own cars, on mileage on set patrols that covered huge areas,' he told me:

> I remember I used to do about 100 miles a night. We had to visit all sorts of places where prostitutes would take their clients. I remember one was called Gobblers' Gulch down by the river. Our job was to note cars with one male; these were then followed up by the day-duty. We also spent many hours around Notting Hill, North Kensington and many areas where prostitutes plied their trade. We got to know them very well and we had to note who their customers were.

At least Nadin's role had a happy ending; he earned so much on this enquiry that he was able to put down a deposit on a house.

Bryan Martin recalled:

> I was allocated a woman officer who was a car driver and I was the observer. Our patch included the Duke's Meadows at Chiswick; we would drive in with headlights on and record the car numbers of those in place. This was awkward as the headlights picked out various stages of intimacy. The WPC appeared embarrassed and turned out the lights. It took a while to get her accustomed to what was going on, so that the car numbers could be recorded. Accuracy was important; many of those recorded disputed they were there.

Roger Crowhurst, then an aid to CID at Chelsea, remembered:

Our actions were shared out and I was probably given the worst of these. I was to arrange with Lambeth Garage the procurement of a nondescript van and a civilian driver and then to make our way to Ealing Common, miles from our patch. Our hours would be from 6 p.m. until dawn the following day and until further notice. We were supplied with a large grey van, about the size of a Ford Transit, stickered up with a bread company's logo; Hovis, I think it was. At intervals along both sides of it, tiny slits were cut through the thin metal, disguised mainly by the logo stickers, and it was through these that we had to observe. The total equipment consisted of a simple force radio bolted to a steel shelf and one old metal garden seat. The 'toilet' was a steel bucket behind a steel bulkhead. There was no heating and we soon borrowed blankets from the local section house to wrap ourselves in. Once at the Common, my job was to befriend all the prostitutes working there and to gain their confidence, which, owing to the fact that they were scared stiff of being murdered in the execution of their profession, was reasonably easy to achieve. A few of the girls were very attractive but in the main, they were ugly buggers. There was really only one nasty one, aged about 30 years and with sharp features and a sharper tongue. We nicknamed her The Fucking Witch. The girls told me she was a dedicated lesbian, carried a cut-throat in her bag and a sharpened steel handle on a sharpened steel comb. She and I had a mutual dislike of each other, told me regularly to 'fuck off, Filth', refused to co-operate in any way and unfortunately, didn't get murdered, either … . The girls (toms, we called them) had a dedicated car park pick-up area for clients and that is where we placed the van each day. Each evening, they came to the back of the van where we were hidden, tapped three times on the door and registered their details. We called their clients 'punters' and through the slits we would watch them as they circled the area in their cars, vans and lorries as we judiciously recorded their number plates. Then we would watch as the girls bartered a price with each man. Usually, they would get in the car and then drive off to a quieter area of choice, but sometimes they would fuck right alongside us and naked, too. The Fucking Witch was keen on doing this, of course. As the clients left with the girls we would note their names and nicknames, the time they left and the time they returned, a description if possible of the client and their registration plate. We counted them all out and we counted them all back …

One officer was paired with a woman officer during these observations and her boyfriend, who was also a local uniformed police officer, was errone-ously convinced that they were taking this heaven-sent opportunity to have an affair. One night when the officers were carrying out their obser-vation at Duke's Meadows, the emotions of the boyfriend boiled over and, in an Othello-like moment, he leapt into the station van and with head-lights blazing and blue light flashing, roared into Gobbler's Gulch. With the exception of the guiltless male officer on observation, this undoubtedly resulted in sudden and painful impotence of many of the males in the immediate vicinity and the jealous officer was duly upbraided and directed to return to the station, driving at a far more respectable speed in a built-up area, with headlights dipped and the blue light firmly extinguished. History does not record if his liaison with the chaste woman police officer prospered thereafter.

If a man – or vehicle – was seen loitering in a secluded spot or cul-de-sac, did this mean that the murderer was waiting for an opportune moment to dispose of yet another body? No chances were taken and men in these circumstances were stopped, questioned and their vehicles checked.

Terry Babbidge recalled being called to Duke's Meadows by a prostitute who claimed she had refused to fellate a lieutenant in the United States Army because his penis was too big and who had pushed her out of the car and driven off. Rather than draw attention to a possible suspect, it was far more likely that the reason for the prostitute calling the police was because she had left her handbag in the car; the officer was traced and questioned, the handbag was restored to its lawful owner and the lieutenant was returned from his tour of duty in England to the United States, rather quicker than he had anticipated.

This area of London was effectively 'shut-down' during the hours of darkness; every conceivable avenue of entry and exit was the subject of observation and investigation. And as well as the officers employed on this task who were instructed to report anything, no matter how remotely suspicious and innocuous, on the instructions of the commander of

No. 1 District, all night-duty uniform beats were to be covered as full as possible. Those officers were also issued with pro formas on which they noted the details of vehicles they saw at night; these completed forms were handed in at their respective stations as they went off-duty to be collected by a murder squad officer each morning.

Prior to taking up their patrols at night, officers – and this included women officers, on both day and night-duty – were instructed to visit public houses (particularly near to closing time) as well as cafés and clubs used by prostitutes in these areas, in addition to the then popular coffee bars and clubs in the Soho area. It produced much useful data. Information was also forthcoming from the local vice squads at Notting Hill and Shepherd's Bush; in fact, any intelligence was recorded, actioned and filed.

Kenny Bowerman was an aid to CID, aged 26 and recently married, when he was instructed to report to DCI Brian Kelly at City Road police station. 'What do you know about prostitutes?' he demanded abruptly and Bowerman, perhaps fearing a loyalty-type question, answered apprehensively, 'I don't know any personally, Sir.'

'Well, you soon will; you're being posted to the nude murder squad at Shepherd's Bush. They want young men of your age group to get these girls to talk,' replied Kelly and if Bowerman thought that this was going to be a clandestine operation, he was wrong. '70 join in killer hunt – Get girls to talk order' proclaimed the *Daily Sketch*, which gave as comprehensive a briefing as Bowerman would receive upon arrival at the squad office. Bowerman told me:

We had to be at a certain point to be seen twice during the night by the night-duty CID officer. Other than that, we were left to our own devices. I was authorised to use my own car on duty; it was a flash white Fiat that stuck out like a sore thumb. One of our usual points was to park in the Queensway or the Notting Hill area. Many of the girls soon recognised the car and would get in for a chat as soon as we pulled up. While the investigation was going on, the girls were immune from being prosecuted and they realised they did not need their pimps so much, as we were looking after them! When asking the girls for any weird or violent clients, I was amazed by what some men would get up to, to satisfy their needs; I couldn't possibly put this in writing. Then, on the other hand, one punter used to pay good money just so that he could comb the girl's hair! One particular brass with a fabulous figure we would meet in the Wimpy Bar and when she strutted out into Queensway in her short skirt and high heels, cars were screeching to a halt to get to her first. Sometimes the girls would bring fast food to our car but we weren't sure if this was living off immoral earnings and who was looking after who!

Bowerman's devotion to duty was rewarded the following year, not in respect of this particular enquiry but for his part in the arrest of the highly dangerous gunman Walter 'Angel-Face' Probyn, for which he was awarded the George Medal.

Brian Baister was an aid to CID who, on a rare night off, had arranged to meet friends, together with his current girlfriend at the Catherine Wheel public house, at the bottom of Kensington Church Street:

This was one of the static observation points that we manned and, of course, the girls got to know our names. This particular girlfriend was very snooty and had already noticed 'these disgusting women'. When a couple of them called out my name and approached me with a list of car numbers that they had noted down that night, that was the end of another opportunity to marry into a moneyed family.

However, like most enterprising CID officers, he managed to rise above what turned out to be a minor setback and retired as deputy chief constable of Cheshire Constabulary with an MA and a Queen's Police Medal.

There were glimpses of black humour, in common with people who have chosen perilous professions; in this case, both the police and the prostitutes. Whenever it appeared that the squad might be running down, with the 'special occasion' dispensation being lifted and a consequent fall in income, some wag on the team suggested going out to murder another prostitute, to keep the enquiry and the enhanced wages going. The prostitutes, on the other hand, started running a book to see which of their number would be the next victim. It was comments like these which lightened what was otherwise a very grim situation.

So there were several such light-hearted moments on the night-duty squad; and one incident was so disgraceful that several members of that squad repeated it to me.

One night, a Welsh aid to CID entered the office, clutching a telegram and obviously distressed; it transpired that his girlfriend had been involved in a fatal car crash in Wales and her funeral was scheduled for later that week. The Metropolitan Police, despite its faults, has always enjoyed a strong commitment to officers in trouble and this was certainly no exception. DI Oxford immediately granted the officer compassionate leave and although the officer wanted to drive to Wales, Oxford, feeling that he was too emotionally upset, wouldn't hear of it. There was an office whip-round, £50 was soon accumulated, which was handed to the officer, and he was driven to Paddington and put on a train. The following day, it was decided that a wreath from the murder squad should be sent to the funeral; a phone call was made to the Welsh Constabulary to determine where the funeral would be held. This resulted in the first question mark being raised. Not only had the constabulary no idea of when the funeral would be held, no fatal accidents had been reported recently. The next query that arose was when the father of one of the squad's officers was consulted. He was a security officer at the same company that employed the officer's girlfriend; he was able to report that the girlfriend was not dead, not even unwell, since he could see her quite clearly, merrily working away in the typing pool.

The whole office was furious, especially after a search of the room in the section house of the distressed officer revealed several blank and half-composed telegram forms, together with a John Bull printing outfit. Several nights later, the errant officer, eyes still red-rimmed, returned to the office, an office simmering with resentment, where the personnel had been sworn to silence.

'How did the funeral go, Taff?' asked Oxford.

'Very well thank you, Guv,' he replied. 'It was lovely, lovely.'

Oxford told him that since he was still obviously upset, he should stay in the office that night, but that Du Rose would wish to see him the following day. Asked why, Oxford replied, 'I think you'll be going on a board.'

The officer brightened up immediately. To be going on a selection board for the rank of detective constable was the dream of every aid to CID.

However, this was not exactly what Du Rose had in mind; the board that he envisaged was a discipline board and that was what was made quite clear to the officer the following day when Du Rose handed him two documents; one a disciplinary form, the other a resignation form. With his customary bluntness, Du Rose told him, 'Take your pick; it's up to you,' and, seeing the writing on the wall, the officer acted with far more common sense than he had previously displayed and resigned on the spot.

★★★

So, of the 785 square miles that were policed in the capital, this was the 24 square miles of London where at least six – maybe more – murder victims had been found and it was saturated with coppers. In fact, quite apart from keeping observation and intelligence gathering, fifty-nine arrests were carried out by the night-duty squad for robbery, larceny, taking and driving away motor vehicles and possessing offensive weapons. What else could Du Rose do to catch the murderer? Quite a lot, as it happens.

24 SQUARE MILES OF SEARCHES – PLUS DECOYS

I t was utterly essential to find the spot where the last four victims were kept prior to their bodies being dumped and a squad of officers were detailed for this task.

Therefore, on 8 March 1965, six CID officers, eight aids to CID and three officers in uniform, were split into three teams, each team having a uniformed officer attached to it. Their task was to visit every street in a specific area, call at every residence and building and examine any room, shed or garage where a body could be stored. In addition, they were to examine lock-up garages, empty shops and any building where paint spraying took place. In these premises, samples of dust and debris were to be obtained and submitted to the laboratory for examination. Any suspicious circumstances or property that was discovered were to be referred back to the murder squad to become the subject of a special enquiry.

There is a matter that needs to be stressed. At that time, police had no peremptory rights to enter premises to collect dust samples for evidence. Yes, if they suspected that stolen property, drugs or firearms were in a premises they could, of course, request a search warrant but it was not until The Police and Criminal Evidence Act 1984 was placed on the statute books that police officers could apply for a warrant to search a house purely for evidence. So in those days of the Stripper investigation, a great deal of tact was needed by the officers wishing to obtain the dust samples – tact, and perhaps a little guile, as well.

The enquiry encompassed parts of the Royal Borough of Kensington and the Greater London Boroughs of Paddington, Hammersmith and Fulham, Ealing and Hounslow. It was decided to start well east of the 'pick-up' area in Paddington and work west.

It appeared that this was a colossal enquiry for just seventeen officers and so it was. In all, 648 streets were visited and approximately 120,000 people were seen. Matters were made slightly easier by the officers receiving the utmost co-operation from members of the public, the various local authorities, estate agents and the keyholders of empty premises. Matters were made slightly worse by the fact that some premises were unoccupied and the owners or renters had to be traced back. Some of the occupants were on holiday, had left to live elsewhere or had gone abroad and others were simply not available to be interviewed because they were at work; they had to be revisited in the evening.

Even so, only half of the area that should have been covered was completed – some 12 square miles. Dust samples from some 500 likely storage places were forwarded to the laboratory – but none proved to be positive. As the picture developed, it was felt necessary that the enquiries should cover the whole area patrolled by the night-duty squad but due to the shortage of staff on divisions and the return of officers engaged on this enquiry, matters came to a halt on 28 August 1965.

On 17 March, the Assistant Commissioner (Crime) Sir Ranulph Bacon made an appeal for information on the ITA programme *Newsweek*:

Among those of you who are watching this programme may be at least one who knew or suspected the person responsible for the six nude murders in the past twelve months. If so, I am speaking directly and personally to you. It may be because of your affection for this person or because of a misconceived sense of loyalty that you hesitate. But the means of bringing to notice the identity of this person concerned lies within your power. I expect you must be a very worried person. Should you fail to carry out this moral and public duty there would rest on your conscience the possible death of yet another young woman.

The following morning, this forthright and well-constructed appeal was taken up by the national press and other appeals for assistance were made from time to time at press conferences at Shepherd's Bush police station. Although this resulted in worldwide coverage in the foreign press and magazines, no one came forward to name the killer.

Until 15 March, only one woman CID officer and four uniform women officers had been engaged on these enquiries but now their numbers increased substantially. DCI Win Harrison (later Taylor) was put in charge with DI Daisy Mason, plus there were two detective sergeants, two detective constables and thirty-six uniform constables working in plain clothes. Additionally, thirty-seven women special constables gave up their evenings to deal with the enormous amount of clerical work.

A number of these women officers collated the motor vehicle index with the details of cars passed to them from the night-duty patrols. Jeannette MacGeorge was then WPC 357'L' Durrant and – very unfairly – described herself to me as being 'only a drone hidden in the library' as she collated, indexed and cross-referenced cards 'as the statements poured in relating to house-to-house and van owners. There were so many coppers around, they drafted in extra staff for the canteen and we ate in shifts.'

Also from this date, a number of women CID officers were tasked with tracing missing prostitutes who, it was thought, might be potential victims in the event of another murder. Therefore, police stations in and around west London were contacted to notify the enquiry team of prostitutes who had gone missing; additionally contact was made with publicans, café proprietors and club owners, as well as prostitutes and known ponces, to inform the office immediately if any prostitute disappeared from her known haunts. All pertinent information was funnelled into the Missing Prostitutes Index. Later, the scope of the enquiry was expanded to trace likely suspects, especially those who had gone missing since the last murder plus those who had attempted or committed suicide.

Returning to the missing prostitutes, much of the information given was misleading or false and was not helped by the number of aliases that the prostitutes used; one of them who was on the missing list used ten different names.

Enquiries were also hampered when little or no genuine information was available from the outset. On 22 March 1965, information was given to the team that a girl, known only to the informant as Sandra, had been missing since 4 March. In an incredibly short space of time, she was identified correctly – Sandra was not her baptismal name – and since she had attended the outpatients department at St Mary's Hospital, Paddington, during the material time she could be crossed off the missing list.

And on 1 April 1965, a certain Daniel Defoe (yes, really) reported that the woman with whom he had been living in Notting Hill had upped and left him the previous day. It appeared they were not terribly well acquainted; he could only provide a sparse description of her, plus the fact he knew her as Christine and that she was in possession of a white poodle.

Armed with this paucity of information, enquiries were made throughout London and the Home Counties; they resulted in identifying her as someone who used the name Christine purely as an alias (with six different, and just as bogus surnames) but, as her foster parents explained, they had not seen her for the previous twelve months and neither had her daughter, who was in care in Middlesex and who was just approaching her third birthday. She was finally traced to McGregor Road, W11, about 250 yards away from where she had been domiciled with Mr Defoe. Following her departure from him, she had moved in almost immediately with another black man but remained there only for nine days. However, she returned to McGregor Road on 22 April and there was an unhappy scene between her and the present occupant's paramour; they were well-known to each other and had disagreed acrimoniously only the previous week. Therefore, she, too could be crossed off the missing persons list; her present whereabouts were not known, and even if they had been they would not have been imparted to Mr Defoe since the Metropolitan Police were not running a free private detective agency for his benefit.

The whereabouts of twenty-nine missing girls was sought; twenty-two were found in a very short space of time, some of them outside the boundaries of the Metropolitan Police District and one in Blackpool.

One girl who was causing police concern had been missing since 4 March 1965; after her identikit picture received a great deal of press and media coverage, she was recognised at a public house in Brixton on 21 March. It is likely that her missing front teeth, cleft palate and stutter aided her identification. Of the other remaining six, they simply did not want to be found; two of them because they had found fresh paramours, three who were arrested for different offences and the remaining girl was found to be alive and well but had absconded since a warrant for her arrest was in existence.

However, it must not be thought that all the women police officers were put on sedentary duties because they were not. Volunteers were called for to form a special decoy patrol.

★★★

From 22 March 1965 and for the next three months, a woman detective sergeant, two women detective constables and nine women police constables commenced this very hazardous duty. WDC Merle May Taylor from the Flying Squad was the first to volunteer and the girls worked in pairs, mainly in Westbourne Grove, Pembridge Road and the Shepherd's Bush Green areas, all frequented by prostitutes.

'I was WPC 195'B' from Gerald Road at the time,' Jane Rogers told me. 'We took turns acting as decoys out on the street and soliciting for customers. We did a week with a girl who had done the previous week, then on week two we took a new girl with us to learn the ropes. I "solicited" along Queensway, Holland Park and Kensington Church Street. I did have a sort of protection from a "drunk" (in fact, a police officer) in a doorway.'

They dressed for the part. 'We didn't get any allowance for special clothes,' said Jane. 'We just tried to look a bit tarty.'

Janet Cheal (then WPC 214'R' Ingram) agreed. 'We had to dress in a certain way to look tarty and provocative,' she told me, adding, 'which, for most of us wasn't the normal way of things.'

Each pair worked in conjunction with male officers in radio-equipped cars. The object was for the women officers to stand about the street without apparently attempting to solicit but nevertheless at times there were queues of men waiting to talk to them; often there was a continuous line of cars crawling from one end of the street to the other. When approached by clients, the officers would chat to them to obtain information that might lead to a possible suspect; under no circumstances were they to get into the punter's car. They had to note the vehicle's registration number, description of the occupants and any conversation likely to assist the enquiry. As Baldock rather quaintly noted, 'In many cases the men were obviously very excited and in several instances had even started a sexual motion when talking to "the girls" but any embarrassment had to be quickly avoided.'

'I was never frightened at all but there were several amusing incidents,' said Jane Rogers. 'Being a girl brought up to be polite, when the first car drew up, I leant in and said, "Can I help you?"' She was a little perturbed when the driver leered at her and replied, 'I 'ope so, darlin'!'

It became clear, even from a short conversation, if the punters had a premises to go to or if they preferred to take the girl to a quiet spot. A number referred to their perversions, some of which were considered to be quite shocking and others revolting. One wanted to watch the two decoy officers having sex, others wanted to be whipped by or, conversely, whip the decoys and one sad soul was willing to pay a fiver to watch a decoy as she took a bath. Some quick thinking was required from the decoy officers to dismiss the punter without arousing suspicion. 'There were cars with diplomatic plates wanting two girls,' recalled Jane Rogers. 'Our main role was to get rid of the punters once they had approached us so we had several excuses like "I don't have a room" or "You'll have to take the two of us".' Whenever an officer was under pressure from a persistent client, one of the male officers would intervene; he was invariably thought to be a ponce.

This was a ploy that was most useful when an aggressive black and very insistent punter tried to drag WPC 447 'C' Purvis into his large, pink Vauxhall Cresta. Her 'minder', David Woodland, rushed across the road and pulled her away; the thwarted punter strode meaningfully and threatening towards him and collected a crippling left hook to the solar plexus. Shouting, 'White ponce! White ponce! I'm reporting you to the police!' (which, as Woodland later commented, he thought was 'rather rich'), he drove off in the direction of Paddington Green police station. It did him little good; the aggrieved, would-be kidnapper caused such a fuss at the police station that he was dragged over the counter and charged under the Metropolitan Police Act, 1839 with 'violent behaviour in a police station' – it only attracted a £2 fine but a salutary lesson was learned.

'I don't remember feeling particularly scared because we knew we had back-up,' recalled Janet Cheal. Additionally, it was essential that the punters' suspicions should not be aroused by the decoy officers refusing all their offers so it was arranged that a male officer would attend the scene in his own car, approach one of the decoy officers as if he were a client and drive off with her for a short while. Meanwhile, close observation would be kept on the remaining decoy officer.

During the time of these patrols, a dozen taxi drivers approached the decoys plus a number of black punters who offered £5 and a hotel room to stay all night. There were also consistent punters who would be out almost every night and some travelled around all the areas policed by the decoys. 'I think a few of the regular punters got wise to us eventually but I guess they were not the murderer so it was probably quite amusing for them to see us operating, if you see what I mean,' Janet Cheal told me, adding, 'From their point of view, that is.'

The taking of notes proved to be most difficult as the decoys could not be seen to be writing. According to later press reports, tiny microphones were concealed in their clothing and the details of the vehicles and suspects were surreptitiously tape-recorded. A nice idea, but pure press hyperbole – the Met was not *that* advanced. Where possible, this was done by scribbling down the details on a scrap of paper inside their coat pockets and then transferred to a Decoy Sheet later. 'I had a small notebook and a pencil in my pocket where I had to write down the index numbers of the cars which stopped to proposition me,' said Jane Rogers.

'We did engage in some conversation with the kerb-crawlers, such as "what're you looking for?" and where we would "do the business",' recalled Janet Cheal. 'But then we had to back out and say we'd changed our minds while making assessments of them, very briefly. We used to write the car numbers down somehow by writing inside our pockets.' Additionally, vehicle particulars were noted by male officers on protection duty.

The work of the decoys caused no comment among the prostitutes soliciting in these areas (providing, of course that the decoys didn't encroach upon their 'beat') and they were initially unaware that they were police officers. Later many became friendly and provided pertinent information to their law-abiding counterparts.

When the decoy squad was disbanded on 18 June 1965, Jane Rogers recalled, 'Daisy Mason presented all of us girls with a hand-made scroll thanking each of us. It read: "Well done, thou good and faithful servant. Thou hast served the Murder Squad well" and each scroll had a silver milk bottle top stapled on it with a little ribbon.'

As Janet Cheal remarked wryly, 'A lot different from being a young uniform WPC, but an interesting introduction to joining the CID!'

THE SOURCE OF THE PAINT DEPOSITS

The work was unrelenting and, it seemed, endless. Eleven women police officers under the direction of DS Sillwood searched diligently and laboriously through the motor registration files and extracted from them the files relating to Hillman Husky and Commer Cob vans that had featured in the Barthelemy and Fleming investigations. Every day Sillwood took the details of these vehicles, showing the names and addresses of the registered owners as well as the type and colour of the vehicles, to the murder squad at Shepherd's Bush. There, they were examined in detail.

Finally, an action list was prepared. Officers employed on outside enquiries – these amounted to nine CID officers and three aids to CID, plus for a period of ten weeks, four Flying Squad officers – were given a copy of the action and then visited and interviewed the persons who were in possession of the vehicles between April and July 1964. A dust sample was obtained from the boot and the interior of the vehicle, plus full details of the driver/owner and the following questions were asked: Was the vehicle used in west London between midnight and 7 a.m.? What were the home circumstances of the owner/driver? Was there a garage and, if so, did paint spraying take place there?

If there was a garage or a place where the vehicle was kept routinely, these areas, too, were inspected. Where it was necessary, the person would be seen again and questioned further. When it was found the owners had moved to other parts of the Metropolitan Police District, local officers had pro formas forwarded to them for further investigation and the same applied when the owners had moved to different parts of the country.

Out of the 1.6 million files housed at the London and Middlesex County Council offices *alone*, in the thirteen months that the enquiry lasted, just 783 Hillman Husky and Commer Cobs were traced, dust samples obtained and the drivers questioned. None were found to be involved; and there were still details of more of these vehicles that were still buried within this mountain of files. They would never be found.

Although the women officers were dubbed the Husky Team, their work was not restricted to the search for those vehicles. In addition, there was the flood of vehicle details that were now coming in from the night-duty patrols.

Bryan Martin was one of the officers who had a multiplicity of tasks; he was one of the night-duty patrols, he manned the radio and while he was doing this, he had to check names on a list left for him to approach Criminal Records Office and draw the files. 'The patrols ended at 6 a.m. and went home,' he told me. 'Then, as office staff, we spent the next couple of hours checking the files received from the overnight dispatch vans, ready for the day staff. We also prepared a log of events, arrests etc. and also collated the lists of car numbers.'

In fact, this index was consulted by CID officers not connected with the enquiry but who were 'those left behind'; officers on routine duties at divisional police stations who used the index to see if it could assist with suspects for night-time offences they were investigating. It was considered, with considerable justification, that this was a badly needed source for criminal investigation. It led to the collators' system of criminal intelligence in individual police stations two years later and this thankfully replaced the dusty collection of Books 28 that reposed in CID offices and displayed photographs of criminals, usually unrecognisable because they were twenty to thirty years out of date and contained seriously unhelpful information, such as 'wears a Ronald Colman moustache' or 'is a well-known chicken thief'.

The squad's car index now contained details of 300,000 vehicles. For the moment, we must leave those eleven, unfortunate women officers encased in an avalanche of files, as we must the night-duty patrols and those officers carrying out house-to-house enquiries. It is time to focus on those officers employed on what was termed 'general enquiries'.

★★★

These officers followed up the mass of information, not only gathered by themselves but also other investigating officers, plus letters and telephone calls from members of the public. They interviewed all the prostitutes who had complained of being attacked by their clients and pursued these complaints to their conclusion. Every police station had a Book 66 – it was colloquially known as a 'Stop Book' – in which were recorded details of persons stopped in the street in suspicious circumstances. Every Stop Book from 'B', 'D', 'F', 'T' & 'X' Divisions – seventy-three of them – covering the period from 1 December 1963 to 1 March 1965, were scrutinised for persons stopped at night during times material to the murders (either on foot or in vehicles) and out of the thousands of persons contained in those books, possible suspects were seen, questioned and their stories checked.

Out of the vehicles spotted by the night-duty patrols, approximately 1,700 drivers were seen. Of necessity, these enquiries required tactful handling. Few of the men were working class types; the majority were professional men, barristers, solicitors, doctors, clergymen and company directors. As David Parkinson, who spent the daylight hours obtaining paint samples from spray shops ('there were bloody hundreds!') and the evenings interviewing the kerb-crawlers, recalled, 'There were some tasty names in that lot.' Usually the line of questioning would be, 'Your car was said to have been involved in an accident; would you mind if we took a look at your car – can you show us?' And to the man's wife, 'No need to disturb yourself, Madam – we won't be long with your husband.' Then, out of the wife's earshot, the true nature of the enquiry could be explained to the husband.

Everything was done to avoid embarrassment to all parties; confrontation and anger is not conducive to a delicate murder enquiry, especially if the person being interviewed is suspected of being a drooling, kerb-crawling pervert.

Sometimes – not often – the person concerned did nothing whatsoever to help himself, pompously exclaiming, 'If you've anything to say to me, you can say it in front of my wife; we have no secrets!'

In those circumstances and when all other avenues to ensure co-operation had been exhausted, the questioning would continue along these lines: 'In that case, Sir, perhaps you can explain how a man answering your description and driving your car, tried to drag a prostitute into your car, in Queensway, last Saturday night?'

This did not occur very often; and since this line of questioning would not have led to continued marital harmony, it was just as well.

It could be said that in such a sensitive enquiry there would be complaints and so there were, but out of all of the persons interviewed, only two were recorded. One was an antiques dealer who, perhaps unsurprisingly, was affiliated to the National Council for Civil Liberties (NCCL). He was questioned since he had been seen kerb-crawling along Kensington Church Street late at night and complained about questions that he described as being 'impertinent' and objected at being asked to make a statement. It is not known if the NCCL backed him in his complaint because in regard to matters of sexuality, it focused its attention on children, in which it actively encouraged incest and advocated abolishing the age of consent for sexual intercourse. Therefore, if it was approached by the antiques dealer for its patronage, it may have considered his case to be pretty small beer. But whatever the case, the complaint was recorded as 'unsubstantiated'.

The second was from a woman, described as 'neurotic and eccentric', who complained that the officers had inferred that her husband was leading 'a double life'. The complaint was withdrawn.

Altogether, 2,500 statements were obtained by the officers on general enquiries. They also carried out 82,000 searches at the Criminal Records Office and at General Registry – where all correspondence relating to the Metropolitan Police was housed – 41,000 searches were carried out.

Meanwhile, 'John Du Rose who spends a large part of his day pacing his eight by ten foot office in nearby Shepherd's Bush police station', informed the readers of Nova Scotia's *Cape Breton Post*, under the headline, 'Prostitutes co-operating with Police – at least six prostitutes have joined Scotland Yard's payroll as informers', that, 'I cannot stress too much that the murderer may be living next door to you. He could be the man who slips out late at night. He could be living a normal life most of the time.'

Of course, there was also the rest of the time when, quite conspicuously, he was not.

★★★

And now, it is time to return to the traces of paint that were found on the bodies of the last four murder victims; it is possible that similar paint traces may have been present on the bodies of Tailford and Lockwood and had been washed off prior to their bodies being recovered from the River Thames. This, of course, is highly speculative but whether or not such traces existed, the investigators felt that other similarities unconnected with forensic scientific analysis were so numerous – the victims being all prostitutes, teeth and clothes missing and the marks on the throats of Figg, Barthelemy, Fleming and O'Hara being identical – that all six victims died by the same hand.

As already mentioned, initial analysis showed that the tiny paint globules on the bodies were predominantly black, although there were other colours as well; red was more predominant than the others, but there were also traces of turquoise blue, brown, cream or white, and in the case of O'Hara, a very small amount of yellow.

Nevertheless, it was thought that the residue on the bodies must have come from somewhere where paint was sprayed; either a private garage or, at the most a very small paint spraying concern, where only the owner of such a premises would have access. Certainly, it could not be a garage that employed several people for the simple reason they would very soon be aware of a dead body on the premises. In all, 3,100 samples had been taken from different parts of the 24-square-mile search area, as well as some outside, but none had been found to be identical. Unfortunately, it had all been a waste of time.

It was only after this enormous slice of police time and resources had been employed that, as a result of a special examination performed by the scientific apparatus department at Associated Electrical Industries, Manchester, it was discovered that the black coloured material was only

Detective Chief Superintendent John Du Rose.

Detective Superintendent Bill Baldock; Detective Superintendent Maurice Osborn.

From left to right: Detective Inspector Ted Crabb, DCS John Du Rose, Detective Superintendent Bill Baldock and Detective Inspector Ken Oxford.

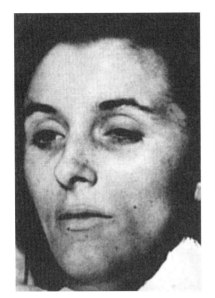

Elizabeth Figg; Gwynneth Rees.

Hannah Tailford.

Under the pier at Hammersmith Bridge where Hannah Tailford's body was found.

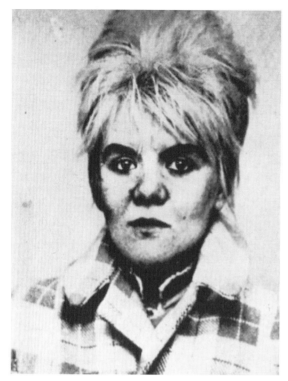

Irene Lockwood.

Kenneth Archibald.

Helene Barthelemy; The rear of 199 Boston Manor Road, Brentford, where Helene Barthelemy's body was found.

The area of Acton Green, Chiswick, where Mary Fleming's body was found; Mary Fleming.

Opposite: Corney Reach, Chiswick, where Irene Lockwood's body was found.

Frances Brown

Horton Street, Kensington, where Frances Brown's body was found.

Bridget O'Hara.

Heron Trading Estate, showing the
Surgical Equipment Supplies Store,
where Bridget O'Hara's body was
found.

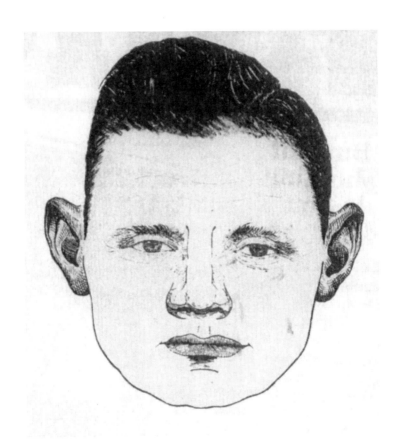

E-fit of Jack the Stripper.

partially paint. The majority of the substance was carbonaceous material, i.e. it contained coal or charcoal, and that in addition, there were fragments of brass and aluminium, rust, cement, possibly plaster particles and general mineral grit.

All, however was not lost; further tests had been carried out on O'Hara's body and as a result, on 6 May 1965, enquiries were centred on the Heron Trading Estate. The reason was this; while the paint globules found on the four bodies were identical, dust found at the scenes of where the corpses of Barthelemy, Fleming and Brown were discovered was completely dissimilar to the debris found on their bodies. However, in O'Hara's case, the paint and dust on her body *and* the paint and dust on the vegetation at the scene were identical; therefore, the storage area for her body and the dumping ground must have been in very close proximity to each other.

It was now clear that the bodies of at least four of the victims: Barthelemy, Fleming, Brown and O'Hara, had all at some time been stored somewhere at the Heron Trading Estate. The periods of secreting those bodies varied from about one day to four weeks, with O'Hara's body being so kept for the longest period. And yet the body was in extraordinarily good condition when it was found; how could this be? At the time of both the murder and the discovery of the body, it was winter; during the months of January and February 1965, it was reasonably cold with the temperature averaging 4.69°C. However, given its condition, the body had obviously not been in the open for all of that time; neither had it been deeply frozen.

The left hand and arm had become mummified and various abrasions on that limb had dried and assumed a parchment-like quality. Over a period of four weeks, this condition could have arisen in a cool place or – and this is important – where a constant current of air had passed over it, such as from an air duct in a factory premises. This was supported by the fact that the paint and dust was on most parts of O'Hara's body, particularly the head hair, which was full of that material. And interestingly, the head hair of Barthelemy, Fleming and Brown was also in the same condition, even though their bodies had been secreted for much shorter periods. But where to start?

★★★

The estate contained all the factories south of the Western Avenue, W3, to the railway embankment where the body was discovered. The area was bounded by Dukes Road to the west and Mansfield Road to the east. During the period of the murders, many buildings on the estate had been demolished but nevertheless samples were taken from the remaining thirty-five factories, the sports ground, roadways, open spaces and railway embankments in the estate.

A vacant factory, Napier Aero Engines, revealed samples that were found to be optically positive to those found on the bodies of the victims. The closure of the Napier factory had commenced at the beginning of 1963 and in August of that year there was a full redundancy of the staff. Between then and May 1964, the machinery was gradually cleared away leaving the factory empty. Therefore, it would have been possible – in theory – for Tailford and Lockwood's bodies to have been stored there. When Tailford's body was discovered, it was covered in mud; when the body was hosed down in the mortuary, prior to performing the autopsy, any debris of the type found on the other bodies would have been washed away. Lockwood's body was described as being 'dirty' but it appears that there was no further examination of whatever the debris was on her skin. As mentioned previously, if this had been common or garden dirt, the waters of the Thames would surely have washed this away. But this is supposition; and to cast aspersions on this theory, the amount of time between the disappearance of both Tailford and Lockwood and the finding of their bodies was quite short.

In the same way, Figg can be discounted from being at the Heron Trading Estate; not only was Napiers fully staffed at the time of her death, the time between her murder and the discovery of her body was approximately three hours. Rees, by now, must be considered as a non-starter.

So with the detectives, the scientists and the laboratory staff all homing in on the now deserted Napier Aero Engines factory, let's take a closer look at the premises.

The eastern side of the factory consisted of a number of male toilets, an outbuilding housing transformers, another male toilet, a locked switch room and a boiler house. Positive dust samples were taken from a lamp glass affixed to the outside wall at the south-east extremity of the factory. Approximately 15ft away, in a southerly direction but at ground level, optical positives were found in dust samples taken from a metal pipeline. Further positives were found in the outbuilding that housed the transformers. This building was approximately 40ft from the lamp and a large double door giving access to the factory was secured only by two large sliding bolts; the unsecured factory was made even more vulnerable since many of the windows could not be fastened.

So given that the finding of these positive samples was approximately 150 yards – in a straight line – from where O'Hara's body had been found, and it appeared that the body had lain there for less than a week, it seemed likely that it was the transformer shed that had been used to hide the body. The disused boiler house would also have been an ideal place of conceal-ment. Although the door giving access to the boiler house from the factory appeared to have been kept locked on occasion, access could be gained by means of a metal door, used as a coke chute and accessible from the outside since this was kept permanently unlocked. What appeared to be a pertinent clue was the words 'Abandon hope all who enter here' on the wall; however, enquiries revealed that in all probability, these words were written by a plumber who had died three years earlier. Therefore, the boiler house required a detailed examination but the dust samples obtained from there proved negative.

Samples taken from the switch room, the factory floor and the toilets did not show the same positive results as those in the transformer shed or the site where O'Hara had been found. Also, when other samples on the estate were taken from places further away from Napiers, they revealed a diminishing degree of similarity.

So, as we know, there was little security at Napiers; following the closure of the company it was left unlocked until April 1965, when it was secured with padlocks. Until then, it had been used as a short-cut, a venue for court-ing couples and during the cold winter of 1964–65 it had been used as a car park by employees of the nearby Westland Aircraft Company.

Workmen had cleared part of the factory between 17 November and 24 December 1964. This related to a large corrugated iron shed that stood in front of the southern side of the building, beside the pipe line where the positive samples had been found, and the workmen had asphalted the area; Frances Brown, who was last seen on 23 October and was discovered on

25 November 1964, was there for part of the time; if she had been kept in the transformer shed, the workmen would have had no reason to enter it.

A company that did have reason to enter the shed was C J C Electrical Limited (Cable Joiners) because it had been instructed to remove one of the two transformers from Napier's outbuilding between 25 and 30 January 1965. Therefore, O'Hara – who vanished on 11 January – could not have been there between those dates but she may have been hidden elsewhere (the boiler house, perhaps) prior to the workmen's arrival and was almost certainly there following their departure; hence the telltale paint markings on her body.

If Mrs Schwartz' account was accepted as being correct, regarding the mysterious sounds coming from the murder scene early on the morning of 12 February when it is thought the body was dumped there, this could well have been the case.

So where had the dust samples found in Napiers (and, on the eastern side of the main building, the outbuilding) come from?

Separated by a disused railway line from Napiers at a distance of some 45ft was Messrs Shaw & Kilburn, Motor Engineers and Coach Builders; its spray shops had an extractor fan overlooking the Napier factory. The prevailing south-westerly winds, striking the south-east corner of Napiers, would carry the dust – which was composed of an abundance of the carbonaceous material and paint particles from Shaw & Kilburn's paint shop – straight through the two 6ft by 3ft wire mesh openings of the transformer shed where, even in summer, the sheds were decidedly cool. And the rest of the debris? That came from the Westland Aircraft Factory, a precision casting company. The castings were carried out by pouring molten wax into a split metal die and when cold the wax mould would be removed. The mould would then be dipped into a fluid to give the wax casting a fine finish, after which the mould would be dusted with a fine powder before being placed in a metal canister. Into this a slurry composition was poured that was composed of a fine powder made up into a secret formula used only by that company.

The mould would then be heated and to remove the wax it would be fired in a tunnel furnace. While this was going on, molten metal would be heated and poured into the mould and when it had cooled the mould was broken open to release the castings. Large amounts of dust were created and, by means of extractors, removed from the factory and bagged up for disposal.

The reason for this rather long-winded explanation, is this: examination of the dust found at factories *other* than Napiers showed either just traces of the dust found at Napiers or none at all. However, the dust from the Westland Aircraft Factory contained an abundance of part of the materials, namely brass, aluminium, rust and plaster particles, that fitted exactly with the carbonaceous materials and paint particles samples taken from Shaw and Kilburns – which the wind had blown into Napiers – and on to the victim's bodies. None of the other factories on the estate revealed such similarity.

So this, together with Mrs Schwarz's assertion of the strange happenings on 12 February, was to a certain extent backed up by three employees of the British Broadcasting Company (who had an office on the estate) who recalled seeing women's clothing – dresses, cardigans, petticoats, brassieres and knickers – in a BBC dustbin the previous evening. It was impossible to match these items of clothing with anything worn by O'Hara or any of the other victims. The lorry drivers, employed by Messrs Drinkwaters, who were responsible for clearing the BBC's refuse bins were questioned, as were the staff at the large tip at Gerrards Cross where the bins were emptied. However, despite the area being searched thoroughly, no trace of the clothing was found. Since this information only came to light twenty weeks after the murder, it was hardly surprising.

In view of this discovery, it was decided to interview the whole of the employees – past and present – as well as visitors to the estate. Fifteen CID officers were selected for this mammoth task and initial difficulties, i.e. getting the co-operation of the management and trade union officials to interview the workforce, were overcome. Jane Rogers recalled going to another of the factories, Ultra Electronics, to trawl through its archives for anyone with a criminal record. She was one of four women police officers employed over a period of eight days compiling details of any of the employees, at any of the factories on the estate who had left their employment, since the last murder in February. One theory was that since dumping O'Hara's body, the person responsible was severing his connection with the estate. It was an interesting notion and, as will be seen, it did result in pinpointing one former employee who – in Du Rose's eyes at least, and five years later – would become a possible suspect.

Working on the assumption that O'Hara's body had been kept in a cold place following her death – possibly, initially at least, some venue other than Napiers – special attention was also given to the Union Cold Storage Plant on the estate. It was a large area, only 2 to 3ft high, in complete darkness. It was searched three times, with David Parkinson being, as he told me, 'one of the lucky ones' deputed for the search; nothing of any relevance was found. The chief engineer and his staff, officially responsible for checking the area, were interviewed. So were all the present and past personnel employed there, as well as the drivers of vans responsible for delivering or collecting produce for the plant; none could assist.

During the course of the enquiry, special attention was paid to ten night-duty firemen, employed by the BBC during January and February 1965, especially 64-year-old Sidney Edward Thompson and Horace Edward Huson, aged 59. The latter two had been on duty the night of 15–16 February but neither they, nor any of the eight remaining firemen, could assist in any way.

A former nightwatchman on the estate had become a commissionaire with the BBC on 24 January 1965, just nineteen days before O'Hara's body was found, some 50 yards away from his place of employment. He was interviewed on three occasions because he appeared so nervous, but it was only natural anxiety at being questioned by police; nothing else about his habits or lifestyle was suspicious.

The apprehensive commissionaire was just one of the 6,154 current and 1,060 past employees to be questioned – nothing suspicious was found in their behaviour or their vehicles. Out of the 7,214 people interviewed, there was just one complaint from a man who objected to the line of questioning that was taken; he later withdrew it. Two women police officers checked and recorded details of all vehicles entering and leaving the estate by day; male officers repeated the exercise at night. The fact remained, the estate had been wide open during the hours of darkness for anyone who wanted to carry out any unlawful act.

Quite apart from the factory estate, enquiries were made in the surrounding area, especially public houses, cafés, residences, shops and business houses; but no useful information was gleaned from any of them. Exactly the same applied when the adjoining Park Royal Factory Estate was searched.

What was clear to the exclusion of anything else was that the murderer must have a special and intimate knowledge of the factory estate.

So who could it be? The entire staff of Napiers – past and present – had been questioned, their background checked, their vehicles examined, with a negative result. Not only that but anybody – builders, cleaners, people carrying out renovations to the factory – who had legitimate access to the building were traced, interviewed and, where they owned vehicles, had dust samples taken.

Who else? Someone who had legitimate access to the building? Someone who would have known when contractors would be in the premises and, more importantly, when they wouldn't – someone, for instance, who might have been employed as a security officer?

Or was it perhaps a milkman or a postman? They would certainly have a good knowledge of the area and would be aware that Napiers had closed in 1963. If that were the case they would have to be retired, dismissed or gone on to another occupation; they could hardly transport corpses around, respectively on a milk float or a bicycle's crossbar.

Could it have been a police officer? A local officer would have a precise knowledge of the area and, what was more, he could be in that area without arousing suspicion. Indeed, if that was the area he was supposed to patrol he would have a legitimate reason for being there. But then, the problem of dumping the bodies. In those days – the time before Panda cars – all police vehicles were crewed by more than one officer; and in any event, a marked police vehicle seen in the vicinity of the trading estate and then possibly at the dumping area would be far too chancy. Unless he used his own vehicle when he was off-duty – or even when he was on duty? Or perhaps he'd retired? The possibilities were endless.

Or was it someone who didn't have such legitimate access? Someone who was an opportunist, perhaps a man who had expertise at breaking into premises – a criminal? What – someone who broke into garages, factories, stores – whatever – who was also a murderous, drooling pervert? Doesn't seem likely, does it?

Security guard, postman, milkman, copper, criminal; it's all getting a bit absurd, really.

DEATH BY BLOW-JOB?

We know that the victims were asphyxiated but it is important to know the way in which their actual demise was engineered. Several of the points have been mentioned previously but it is necessary to recap on these matters to get a fuller picture.

All the bodies that had been stripped after death showed no signs of sexual violence, and only in one case – Fleming – was there any signs of physical violence below their necks. The various pathologists believed that asphyxiation had been caused by the victims' clothes being pulled tightly round their throats or the perpetrators hands covering the victim's face or the face and neck. There were slight marks on their necks and faces and it was these marks that were present on four occasions.

However, these marks were of no real depth and Baldock found it difficult to believe that any one or two could, in themselves, have caused death. In fact, most of the marks on the necks appeared to be consistent with the victim's fingers clawing to prevent asphyxiation; but that being said, I could find no evidence of any skin, belonging to the victim (or anybody else) being found under the victim's fingernails.

It appeared that the victims did not struggle right up until the moment of their death; indeed, they were the murderer's willing partners and this seems strange when taking into consideration the victims' natural cunning in these practised situations. Bearing in mind the violent demeanour of the majority of the victims (especially O'Hara) one would have thought that when a situation developed where it was apparent to the victim that danger or discomfort threatened that they would have resisted their attacker strongly; but they did not.

It was Baldock's opinion that the victim was fellating the murderer at the time; this being much in demand (rather than manual masturbation or ordinary intercourse) from what was referred to as 'the low-class prostitute' who worked after midnight in the Notting Hill-Shepherd's Bush area; indeed, there were very few who did not provide this service. He believed that the slight bruising was caused by the face being pressed, from the back of the head, into the perpetrator's lap or knees, since it was believed that the killings took place in the backs of cars. Baldock felt that the marks on the faces and necks of the victims would be consistent with their trying to get to the cause of their distress, yet would be prevented by the man's knees from reaching the obstruction in their throats; and remember, oral swabs often revealed traces of semen.

Death by blow-job? Too far-fetched? This theory has since been met with howls of derision with the most usual mode of dismissing the idea by saying that in order to save herself, the victim would have bitten the perpetrator's penis. However, Baldock expressed the opinion of the difficulties that could be experienced in manipulating the jaw when the mouth and throat were fully occupied, which 'might well prevent this type of defensive action from taking place'.

That's the copper's theory. Let's see what the experts had to say.

Prof. David Aubrey Llewellyn Bowen, FRCP, FRCPE, FRCPath, attended the scene when Bridget O'Hara's body was found and he carried out the autopsy. He stated that there were signs of asphyxia and noted there were many tiny petechial haemorrhages (an escape of blood from a ruptured vessel) present in the upper conjunctival sac (the tear-filled space, lined by conjunctiva, between the eyelids and eyeball) but that there were none on the lower eyelids. He noted that there was a marked congestion throughout the buccal mucosa (the inner lining of the cheeks and lips) with small haemorrhages posteriorly and that there were congestive changes around the epiglottis (the erect cartilage at the root of the tongue, depressed in the act of swallowing to cover the glottis or the opening at the upper part of the windpipe) but no actual bruising.

In his final conclusions, he stated there were signs of asphyxia in the mucus membrane of the chest and eyes and on the lungs, and two small abrasions on the left side of the neck that could have been caused by pressure.

Baldock posed his theory to Doctor (as he then was) Bowen, who agreed that all the signs he found would be consistent with a death in this way. He had not, he admitted, had previous experience of a person dying by this means but he had examined a number of bodies that showed certain similar signs to those in O'Hara's death.

He had in mind the cases of – as they were then described – 'mental defectives' who would push a large object, such as a whole apple, into their mouths and attempt to swallow it; the result was instant asphyxiation with death resulting in five or six seconds. These features he recognised in the examination of O'Hara.

Those were the thoughts of a very eminent pathologist more than fifty years ago. I set out the facts (without the benefits of the pathologist's notes or photographs) to Dr Peter Jerreat, MB, BS, B.Sc., DMJ (Path), Emeritus Home Office Pathologist. He told me:

> Of great importance in any case where there is the possibility of neck com-pression is the deep dissection of the area, Nowadays, this is performed by vascular drainage, first by removal of the brain and trunk organs, up to the upper trachea (a muscular tube from the larynx to the bronchial tubes). This allows a bloodless field and dissection of the neck structures muscle, layer by layer. These are delicate structures and frequently reveal small bruises and fractures to the hyoid bone or thyroid cartilages which would be supportive evidence of a compression of the neck-type death. I started in 1977 and these techniques were not used then and the usual practice was to remove the neck structures in a block, X-ray them and dissect in detail later. As the structures were preserved in formalin, small areas of bleeding could disappear from the action of the formalin.

(In fact, this method was used, with the application of methylated spirits, during the autopsy of Brown; it revealed small abrasions almost identical to those found on O'Hara's neck, with the same cause of death.)

Dr Jerreat also put forward the suggestion that the victim might have saved herself by biting. However, he stated:

> On the information available, these are likely to be asphyxiation-type deaths from compression of the neck and likely to be contributed to by mouth obstruction, which could be manual or by fellatio. The presence of buccal petechiae would be compatible with oral obstruction as well as congestion around the epiglottis. The lack of marks to the neck either from the perpetrator or victim suggests a broader compression of the neck rather than purely manual. Again, this could fit with the supposition of the perpetrator on top of the victim in a fellatio type action.

These opinions I passed on to that superlative SOCO (Scenes of Crime Officer), Paul Millen who, by the time he left the Metropolitan Police for the Surrey Constabulary, was the most commended SOCO in the Met. Coincidentally, he had worked briefly with Prof. Bowen in his later years ('he was a very distinguished man') and also Peter Jerreat, describing him as, 'an eminent pathologist (and police surgeon for that matter). I worked with him a lot on 'G' Division in the early 1980s when I was a young SOCO.'

Asked for his own thoughts on the matter, Millen replied, 'I think the pathologists are saying as much as they can. It is their opinion, based on their experience. But it remains subjective in the absence of other marks or injuries. I think in the main they are at most suggesting that the cause of death was asphyxia due to internal obstruction or broad external compression of the airways. Interesting, the comment about "biting back". Still, we need to keep an open mind, in case we are missing something.'

And that is precisely right – keeping an open mind about all aspects of this investigation. So before we examine the suspects, let's take a look at the type of person likely to be Jack the Stripper.

PROFILE OF A KILLER

I n these present days of the psychological profiling of criminals, I do believe that while the profilers cannot deliver the culprit, gift-wrapped to the investigating team, they can be of immense help to them. This was shown to be the case in 1986 when Dr David Canter, a psychiatrist and criminologist from Surrey University, was invited to compose Britain's first offender profile to catch the man dubbed 'the Railway Killer'. It resulted in the arrest of the culprit with thirteen out of seventeen of Canter's predictions being found to be correct.

However good those theories may be, they really are only a guide. During the Beltway sniper attacks in Washington DC, the offender profiling suggested the sniper was a white male in his thirties from the same area as the shootings, who was acting alone. In fact, the perpetrators were two black men, aged 17 and 41, from America's west coast.

When considering the value of behavioural sciences, psychology and psychiatry in particular (but more generally criminology, sociology, socio-biology, ethnography, demographics, transport and geography), to non-recent investigations, there are some general context and environment aspects to be considered as constraints on the value of what is offered. Much of the history of the use of these sciences derives from what used to be called in the Federal Bureau of Investigation, offender profiling, although the material available came from a very different environment in the United

States, including transport, education and housing infrastructure, all of which could influence the thinking behind the advice.

Of course, fifty years ago at the time of the Stripper murders that took place in dear old Blighty, this expertise was not available; it was left to the investigating officers' deductions. First, Baldock dismissed those who could not be responsible; that no husband, ponce or boyfriend of the victims was culpable, and he also forwarded the concept that, as he put it, 'no coloured person' was associated with the killings.

Baldock believed that the murderer was a person 'of some standing', a professional or an established businessman. He might well be a married man, outwardly living a respectable life; obviously, he would be able to drive a vehicle and either own one or have access to one. He would be careful not to expose his normal activities and would go to some length not to be seen picking up prostitutes. He had been cool and calculating enough to strip the bodies after death – not the easiest of tasks – and although it seemed that he was inclined to panic when depositing the earlier bodies, with the latter victims he was taking more time and care and giving more thought to their disposal.

It was clear that he had a good, working knowledge of the general area of west London but Baldock thought that this might be confined to the main roads (plus, of course, the Heron Trading Estate); all the bodies were discovered just off the main thoroughfares. On this point, I disagree; I believe the perpetrator had an acute knowledge of the areas where the bodies had been found. One example is the murder of Fleming; the killer had been disturbed by the painters when he went to dump her body in the car park of what he obviously thought was the deserted ABC restaurant; he had sufficient knowledge of the area to discard Fleming's corpse in Berrymead Road, a quiet cul-de-sac, and just ten minutes' drive away from the restaurant.

The culprit was out at night during the week but from the days when the victims disappeared not, it appeared, at weekends.

Baldock believed the fact that all the victims had teeth or dentures removed did not necessarily mean the man was connected with the medical profession or dentistry. It might be an attempt to destroy identification or be connected with sexual gratification.

A man with a vendetta against prostitutes was considered and dismissed; if that were the case, surmised Baldock, there would be no need to remove the clothing or teeth or hide the bodies; and what was more, one would expect a savage attack in connection with the deaths.

Lastly, there was the possibility of the killings being the work of a schizophrenic and if sex was not the motivating factor, then it was a desire to be vindictive to society and authority. This, in Baldock's opinion, would be in keeping with the facts of these killings.

Half a century later, I sought the advice on the same subject from another source. Impressing upon me that he is not a chartered psychologist nor an accredited behavioural analyst, nevertheless former Deputy Assistant Commissioner John Grieve, Professor Emeritus, CBE, QPM, BA (Hons), MPhil spent thirty-seven years as a professional investigator in the Criminal Investigation Department of the Metropolitan Police and a further thirteen years as an academic with degrees in psychology, philosophy and policy analysis.

I provided him with a very limited scenario of the killings, encapsulated on one A4-sized page. I dealt with the nature of the killings and the locations of where the bodies were found, the fact the bodies had been stored before being dumped and the missing teeth and clothing. At no time did I mention any of the suspects and, needless to say, Grieve did not have anything like the detailed information available to Baldock or Du Rose. However, he stated quite unequivocally that 'any information from a behavioural advisor has to be assessed in the light of the totality of information and evidence available to the senior investigation officer or the officer in overall command – the task given to John Du Rose.'

Telling me that his contribution 'is of limited value', these are the conclusions that Grieve reached after spending thirty years of reading and/or discussions with the top psychological profilers:

So what sort of persons might have committed these crimes? A man, almost definitely, but a number of cases show up the possibility of female or male accomplices, witting or unwitting, possibly both before and during but most likely, after.

Probably aged between 18 and 55, as a start, 30 to 50 years.

Access to or ownership of a vehicle, possibly an estate car (as hatchbacks were known) or van.

Knowledge of the 'grab points' where the women were propositioned and/or abducted and the locations where the bodies were finally left.

Victims were all small and slight, indicating a possible vulnerability and as sex workers, they are engaged in high-risk behaviour. The offender may not need to be big and strong, he could be insignificant and unassuming.

Access to and knowledge of the paint contaminated region where the bodies were possibly retained. This behaviour suggests voyeurism – looking at naked women and their humiliation.

A possible history of voyeurism – 'peeping Tom' – and other earlier anti-social behaviour.

Cruelty to animals is another possible early indicator.

Geographical analysis, i.e. mapping routes and suggested familiarity would suggest associations along a corridor between the sites. The literature would emphasise the first sites (Question: Is that the 1959 murder or 1964?) and the apparent retention.

A reason for retaining and moving the women and then exposing some of them in the open (for example but not confined to on 'display', indicating motives of hatred, contempt or anger). These crimes are most likely about the use of power over the women. Retention – on the material I have seen – seems to be between a week and five weeks, which makes it highly relevant to his decision making.

I have no definitive answer about the teeth because there is no information in what I read about how they were removed, by force or not, or when, the result of violence whilst being grabbed or restrained, whether the victim was alive or dead. They may be trophies and the murderer may be a 'collector' of such items. The same applies to the clothing and jewellery – they might be trophies of a 'collector' but they may be a means of depersonalising the bodies as part of contempt or hatred. On the other hand, true crime literature/media reports would warn a person of interest of what Locard's Exchange Principle might offer from clothing or fibres snagged on jewellery as forensic evidence. So it might just be a precaution against incriminating evidence.

A reason for the crimes stopping: he goes to prison, he moves a long way away, death, Mental Health Act detention, completion of aims – power, revenge, sexual satisfaction (all unlikely to be satisfied) or the fear of arrest as tactics are publicised.

In conclusion, Grieve stressed that this assessment, 'has to be treated with extreme caution and considered in the light of all other information in this day and age, especially the forensic material that the senior investigating officer has and must be constantly reviewed, updated and re-examined. It becomes one more element in the investigative strategy. It can and should never stand alone.'

★★★

One last word on the type of person likely to have committed the murders. My chum, Jeannette MacGeorge, mentioned to me, 'Let's face it, any pathologist would tell you after a succession of murders by the same perpetrator, he only stops if he has been caught, goes abroad or dies; he never simply gives up.'

Well, for a lay person that's not a bad theory; it's one that always been in the back of my mind and it pretty well fits in with Grieve's hypothesis as well. However, there is a precedent.

Dennis Lynn Rader was known as the BTK Killer – it stands for 'bind, torture, kill' – and between 1974 and 1991 he was responsible for the murder of ten people in and around Wichita, Kansas. He murdered men, women and children – the oldest of his victims was 62, the youngest 9 – and he used a variety of methods for their demise; the most usual was strangulation but he also used suffocation, hanging and stabbing. The tools of his trade were plastic bags, knife, rope, belt, nylon stocking and pantyhose.

During his murderous rampage, Rader (who was married with two children), collected items from each murder scene, including the victim's underwear which he wore himself. During this time, he wrote to both the police and the press, taunting them.

And then, after the last murder in 1991, everything went quiet – no more murders, no more letters. Fifteen years passed and then, in 2004, Rader commenced a series of eleven letters to the local media. Auspicion fell on him and he was finally nailed by means of his DNA. In August 2005, he pleaded guilty to the ten murders, having described them in excruciating detail, without a trace of remorse and since Kansas does not have the death penalty, he was sentenced to ten consecutive life sentences. At the time of writing, Rader is 70 years of age, but be warned: he'll be eligible for parole on 26 February 2180.

So what this shows, if nothing else, is that simply because a serial murderer stops killing, it doesn't mean to say that he's dead.

THE SUSPECTS

Some of the suspects – those interviewed by members of the murder squad – have been dealt with already; what follows are the remaining twenty-two. Some can be dealt with very quickly; others require more investigation. Quite a few of them are dead but whether they are dead or not, I shall not be naming any of them.

Other authors have named some of the remaining suspects; that's their affair. The majority of these names would be unknown to most of the people who read this book, and therefore inclusion of them might lead to some confusion and would certainly unnecessarily clutter up the book. It will become clear that some of the people who were interviewed were named maliciously and after questioning and the checking of an alibi, they were cleared and eliminated from the enquiry. Quite apart from that, I believe it is monstrously unfair to publish the identities of people who, at the time were considered suspects for an atrocious series of murders but because of a paucity of evidence (or no evidence at all) were not charged.

One suspect materialised after the security officer at Ultra Electronics on the Heron Trading Estate informed police that one of the engineers had been seen to deposit cardboard cartons containing particles of burnt material and soil by the company's dustbins. That was strange enough but when enquiries were made into this man's background it was discovered that he had come under suspicion when a director of Diamond Switches (a company based in Acton, where the engineer was then employed) had received a parcel on Christmas Eve 1961. It turned out to be a home-made bomb that exploded in his face, resulting in severe burns. Although he appeared to recover from his injuries, one month after being discharged from hospital, the director committed suicide.

The matter was investigated by officers from Hertfordshire Constabulary, without success. However, if the engineer had been responsible for the bomb making, then such an act was tantamount to murder and therefore of great interest to the murder enquiry team.

Observations were carried out on the man; he left his home in Gunnersbury, W4, each morning at 6.50 a.m. by car, arriving at his place of work ten minutes later. However, he would wait in his car until clocking in time at 7.45 a.m. and then deposit the cardboard boxes by the dustbins afterwards. Arriving so early fuelled the suspicion surrounding the man, because of the time that O'Hara's body had been deposited. Over a period of two weeks, he was seen to deposit nine such boxes. The boxes were seized and taken to the laboratory for analysis; and while the results were awaited, the observations were maintained. The man would drive home for lunch and at the close of day he would return home, on all occasions not stopping. During the evenings, he never went out; he lived at the address with his wife and daughter, with the upstairs part of the property occupied by two young business girls.

Nevertheless, it was necessary to search his premises and on 25 June 1965, it was. Prime consideration was given to ascertaining if the property had been used to store one of the dead bodies and if clothing had been burnt as a means of disposal.

The engineer was interviewed and he gave an explanation as to conveying the cardboard boxes to work; he stated that the cartons had contained bonfire material that he had accumulated over a period of time and the reason for not disposing of the burnt material in his garden was that it had contained glass that would have been dangerous. This was confirmed by the laboratory and its examinations revealed none of the burnt material was relevant to the murdered women. On the four occasions he had left home during the evenings in 1964, none were at the time of the victims' disappearances. His background was further checked and his two absences from work in 1964 and 1965 did not coincide with the missing women. Furthermore, he was not known to associate with women in general or prostitutes in particular and a thorough search of Ultra Electronics revealed nothing to assist the enquiry. Neither was there any evidence to connect him to the home-made bomb that exploded to the detriment of the director of Diamond Switches.

Therefore, he received a clean bill of health, which makes it all the more odd that during his questioning, he appeared extremely disturbed; at times he was completely unable to speak and on two occasions was violently sick. Perhaps he felt he was being unfairly associated or even compared with a former employee of Ultra Electronics. His name was John Reginald Halliday Christie, an ex-War Reserve police officer with previous convictions, and he was hanged after it was established he had asphyxiated at least eight women (some of them prostitutes) from the same area and then hid their bodies. The late Mr Christie and his address at 10 Rillington Place (which was where he conducted his gruesome business) also came to light when investigating the activities of the final suspect, as will be seen; but possibly that was just a coincidence.

Another engineer was brought to notice as a suspect after his arrest on 17 April 1965 for attempted rape. At 1 a.m. on 29 March at Epsom Downs he was with a woman in his green Commer van, threatened her with a knife and attempted to rape her. Found in his van was a mattress and the knife that had been used.

A deeply unsavoury individual, he possessed a previous conviction for indecent assault in this country as well as one in South Africa for a vicious rape and assault with intent to murder, for which he was sentenced to twelve years' hard labour. And if that were not enough, he was put up for identification for an offence of attempted murder and an indecent assault in Mitcham, Surrey; he was not picked out.

His wife was interviewed and although she spoke of her husband's violence towards her and his absence from home on occasional nights, she was unable to provide any information that could link him to the murders.

The engineer was interviewed by DS Allison (who had also interviewed the engineer from Ultra Electronics) and denied any knowledge of the murdered prostitutes. A thorough examination of his Commer van produced nothing of assistance to the murder enquiry and although enquiries revealed he had for short periods worked in the Acton area, there was no trace of his vehicle in the murder squad index. Enquiries were made at car hire companies in and around the area where he lived; none had hired vehicles to him.

Engineers were thick on the ground; the next one was 55 years of age with no previous convictions and came to light when a lady referred to as 'an unconvicted prostitute' (it meant that while not being convicted, she had been cautioned as to her behaviour and therefore her details had been recorded in the index at A4 Department at the Yard) reported that she and other prostitutes had gone to his address and were paid to whip him while he recorded the proceedings on a tape recorder. The engineer sadly admitted his predilections, denied any knowledge of the murdered women and although he was the subject of further enquiries, nothing was forthcoming to connect him with the murders.

A refrigerator engineer came to the attention of the enquiry because during any murder investigation files pertaining to similar enquiries were drawn from the Yard's General Registry for comparison. This one referred to the murder of Ann Noblett, a 17-year-old domestic science student who alighted from a bus near to her home in Marshalls Heath, Hertfordshire, on 30 December 1957 and disappeared. Although the weather had been unusually mild for the time of the year, her frozen body was found in a wood, 7 miles away, one month later, giving rise to the suspicion that her body might have been kept in a deep-freeze. Bizarrely, some of her clothing had been removed after death but then the body had been re-dressed.

Since Ann weighed 11st, whoever had carried her the 300 yards from the road to the woods must have been quite strong or had help; there was no indication that she had been dragged. In fact, this case was linked to a murder investigation being conducted by the Essex Constabulary in the case of Mary Kriek, a 19-year-old Dutch student who had been found battered to death in Boxted one week after the disappearance of Ann Noblett.

Two suspects were arrested at Southend; the refrigeration engineer was one of them and everything pointed to him being the murderer but he was released through lack of evidence.

Shortly after his release, the engineer went to live in Belgium, where he had dual nationality; it saved him from being extradited when it was discovered that he had committed fraud offences at the refrigeration company he had managed at Westcliff-on-Sea, Essex.

Since he possessed a Belgium passport, it was thought that he might have visited Holland and returned to England for short periods without detection and enquiries as to his movements during the two years prior to O'Hara's death were carried out. His photograph was shown to all personnel on the Heron Trading Estate and other likely places in west London, without success. Enquires were carried out by Interpol but by the time the enquiry ended, these, as well as many others, had not been completed. This was understandable. Interpol was known as the White Man's Grave and many of the detectives posted there were not exactly fired with enthusiasm or investigative zeal.

Quite possibly, old scores were paid off. A 40-year-old general dealer from the East End was propped up as a suspect, the result of an anonymous tip-off. Apart from admitting various liaisons with prostitutes, nothing was disclosed that would connect him with the murders.

A middle-aged newsagent from Brighton was checked after his car was noticed during the Husky enquiries. All it revealed was that he occasionally liked to dress in women's clothing, which, to his extreme embarrassment were the subject of careful examination. However, none of the items had belonged to the murder victims.

A stoker employed in the boiler house at a hospital was offered up to the murder squad after a fellow employee informed them of his boasting regarding his associations with prostitutes. One such prostitute was traced and stated that in February 1965 a man – and from her description, it was obviously the stoker – had taken her to the boiler room and for the princely sum of £2 had had intercourse with her and then detained her, against her will. He was seen, his Bedford Utilibrake was searched, he admitted associating with prostitutes from the Shepherd's Bush area and it transpired he had worked previously at the Weston Margarine Company and the Napier Factory, both on the Heron Trading Estate. However, this man who was described as 'a most peculiar individual' could not be connected to any of the murders.

A mortuary attendant who had first come to the attention of police twenty years earlier came to their notice again after a prostitute informed the squad of his peculiar sexual behaviour. On two occasions he had visited her at her home address and had paid her £15 and £25 to sit partially undressed whilst he masturbated. It was his association with the coolness of the mortuary that was the reason for regarding him as a suspect but nothing was found to connect him with the victims. However, the funding for his expensive sessions with the prostitute was questioned, since at that time £40 represented two weeks wages to a semi-skilled worker, and on the day following his interview, he appeared at West London Magistrates' Court where he was fined £10 for stealing hospital equipment and articles from deceased persons.

If the mortuary attendant was an oddity, the next suspect was downright foolish and someone who failed to profit from his past mistakes. His first started when he received his first conviction for crime at just 12 years of age. His next was when he complained to the Notting Hill superintendent about the conduct of a constable who had questioned him when a young girl was accosted in the Bayswater Road, something he denied vehemently. However, enquires revealed that not only had he accosted the girl but that in addition, he was a frequent visitor by car to the Notting Hill and Bayswater districts where he had attracted the ire of several of the local prostitutes when, having acquired their services, refused to pay. There being nothing like a woman (or perhaps, several women) scorned, it was also suggested by the bilked beauties that he was violent and quite capable of murder.

If that were not enough, at the same time he had made a further complaint against a Flying Squad officer who had questioned him about a stolen painting and who, he stated, had stolen money from him. This matter was being investigated by DCI Jack Weisner of C1 Department at the Yard and now, DS Allison of the murder squad joined forces with the chief inspector after a warrant had been issued for the man's arrest, on the instructions of the Director of Public Prosecutions, on charges of criminal libel in respect of the Flying Squad officer. It provided an opportunity to search the man's flat – he did not have a garage or access to one – but the examination of the flat, plus samples taken from his car, all came to nothing. However, the concentrated enquires made about this man, both at his present and previous addresses may have resulted in a certain lowering of his social standing. Some people never learn.

A 36-year-old seaman had been deported from New Zealand, following his conviction for assault on board ship, there; the victim of the assault had told police that prior to their ship sailing from Tilbury, during February 1965, he had been acting very strangely. A deputation from the murder squad was waiting to greet him when his ship docked at Dover but he denied any knowledge of the prostitutes. Moreover, his Seaman's Record Book revealed that during the periods 7 April–9 July 1964 and 1–17 October 1964, the dates relevant to the Barthelemy and Brown murders respectively, he was sailing the high seas.

The manager of a store was serving three months' imprisonment for the offence of larceny servant when he was fingered as being a suspect by a disgruntled employee at the company; he had been heard to boast of visiting clubs in Soho and knowing the murdered prostitutes. A prison visit revealed that the dishonest former manager had embroidered the truth; although he had seen Helene Barthelemy in the Nucleus Club, Monmouth Street, W1, he had never spoken to her and it was only when he saw her photograph in the newspapers that he realised she had been murdered; of the other murder victims, he knew nothing. It was not an entirely wasted journey for the detectives as they received a small but satisfying bonus after the prison inmate admitted selling drinamyl tablets in The Swiss House, Old Compton Street, W1.

A 45-year-old pipe fitter had murdered a prostitute in 1952 and had been convicted, found to be insane, was committed to Broadmoor and released on licence nine years later. Information was received from the Essex Constabulary that the pipe fitter's brother was responsible instead. The court papers were checked and it appeared that the man had been properly convicted. He was seen, dust samples were taken from his car and he and they were found to have nothing to do with the murders. Precisely why the police in Essex thought that this would be of interest to the murder squad is unclear.

Bogus confessions are nothing new in murder investigations; one had already occurred in this investigation with the case of Kenneth Archibald. There was another when a man in custody for robbery in Yorkshire asked to see a solicitor and then confessed to murdering a prostitute named Bridie. He stated he had met her at about 9 p.m. on the evening of 10 February 1965 in Shepherd's Bush and after an altercation in a hired car, he struck and killed her and, having stripped off her clothing, had dumped her body off the Bayswater Road. He was unable to give any further details regarding the hire car, save that it was a Vauxhall and that he had abandoned it somewhere in the centre of London. It appeared he had got his facts rather scrambled from reading newspaper reports. If the Bridie he was referring to was Bridget O'Hara, on the date he mentioned, she had already been dead for a month. No prostitute had been reported as being assaulted and no body, alive or dead had been dumped in the Bayswater Road.

Slightly less convincing was the confession made by a 43-year-old Polish labourer in Cardiff, who talked of killing a woman in London. He was spoken to, rather firmly, by officers from the Cardiff City Police when it was discovered that the drunken outburst was quite without foundation.

Just as false was the suggestion that a 48-year-old bartender had been visited by Bridget O'Hara in his room, had sexual intercourse and that further, he could well have been the man seen with her outside the Shepherd's Bush Hotel at 11 p.m. on 11 January 1965. When he was interviewed, the bartender denied any knowledge of O'Hara or any of the other victims. When further enquiries were made, it revealed that on 11–12 January 1965, he was gainfully employed at his place of work between 4.38 p.m. until 1.11 a.m.

And for the time being, this chapter can be closed having provided accounts of men, some of whom were mad, bad and just plain sad. There will be more of them in the chapter that follows, I assure you.

... AND A FEW MORE SUSPECTS

One of the more extraordinary people to be questioned was a 43-year-old architectural assistant who was interviewed at Shepherd's Bush police station after his vehicle was seen on a number of occasions with the driver soliciting prostitutes in the vicinity of Holland Road.

Many of the men questioned in similar circumstances denied either being there or, if they were, that it was for an innocent purpose and one far different from the one alleged. But not this one. Far from exhibiting any signs of nervousness, not only did he admit being there but in the course of two statements to police (one in the presence of his solicitor) he eagerly admitted picking up prostitutes and taking them to side streets or Duke's Meadows for all sorts of odd sexual practices, all of which he described in graphic detail to the interviewing officers. Not only that, he stated that he had contracted venereal disease on half a dozen occasions and had received treatment for this condition. When enquiries were carried out at the various hospitals, it was confirmed that he had indeed received the appropriate treatment for his various infestations of 'cupid's measles'.

He was shown photographs of the murdered women and he identified O'Hara as a girl he knew as Brenda whom he had encountered on about six occasions; but when further enquiries were made, it became obvious that Brenda was not O'Hara at all. However, he was only too willing to permit his house and car to be searched and this included the taking of dust samples. He could not be connected in any way with the series of murders and, in fact, he named a prostitute with whom he was having a distinctly seedy relationship before and since the O'Hara murder. It is quite possible that the interviewing officers had a job to get rid of him before he explained in salacious detail precisely who did what to whom with his current paramour and Baldock mentioned rather crushingly, 'He is a physical wreck and seems quite incapable of employing sufficient strength to have manually asphyxiated the women by any method.'

A 20-year-old prostitute contacted the police to tell them that she and the murder victim, Frances Brown, had encountered a punter who exhibited peculiar sexual behaviour in the early part of 1964. Describing himself as an airline pilot, the 54-year-old was, in fact, a company director and taking the two women to a flat in a west London apartment block, he asked Brown to undress and then produced what was described as 'a rubber massager', which he asked her to use on him.

After Brown was found murdered, the same man took the other prostitute back to the flat, whereupon he used the massager on himself, she telling the police piously that she refused to take part in the performance.

Interviewed, the company director could do little else than admit that he was indeed the tenant of the flat and, although he admitted taking prostitutes there, he denied knowing Brown or being in the flat with two prostitutes.

It was revealed he was absent from business with a burst ulcer and upon his release from hospital (and on the advice of his doctor) he was chauffeured to and from his office until 20 July 1964. Since this covered the period of 10–14 July 1964, which was when Fleming disappeared and was found murdered, it provided an alibi for that murder and, of course, the others.

Another company director came to notice in rather more sinister circumstances. A prostitute told police that on 5 July 1964 she had been soliciting outside Ladbroke Grove Underground Station when a man pulled up in a blue Vauxhall Victor saloon. There was a discussion about business and he told her that he would pay her more if she would accompany him to a secluded spot that he knew. They drove off towards Chiswick and stopped by the Civil Service Sports Ground, close to the Thames. There, as she rather inelegantly put it, he wanted intercourse 'up the rear' but she refused and normal intercourse took place. As he reached his climax, he put his hands round her throat and started choking her. This, of course, was immensely upsetting for the prostitute. She started crying and then he eased the pressure on her throat, telling her, 'You're too young; I can't do it to you.' By now, he too was weeping and the prostitute asked, 'What do you mean, you can't do it to me?' to which he replied, 'It doesn't matter.'

At this point, she jumped out of the car, noting the vehicle's registration number on a piece of paper, and ran off. The car drove after her, missing her by inches, and then she walked back towards London. En route she saw a police officer but stated that she was 'too frightened' to report the matter to him, but when she did report the incident to the murder squad – and this was some time later, during the Mary Fleming investigation – she described him in detail. She added that he said his name was Paul or John Howard, that he spoke of raping his girlfriend two years earlier and that he had been released from prison the previous summer.

On the basis of this information, enquiries were made immediately that revealed that the Vauxhall Victor was registered to a company director, married with three children and living in Kent, although his real name was, unsurprisingly, nothing like the one he had told the prostitute.

His private and business premises were searched, as was his car, and examined by the laboratory, with a negative result. With the exception of his horn-rimmed glasses, he did not fit the description provided by the prostitute. He gave a statement saying he could not possibly have been the person concerned because on the date given by the prostitute, which was a Sunday, he had taken his daughters to church, returning home at 7.30 p.m. and stayed in for the rest of the evening. This was confirmed by his wife and also a neighbour, who was able to state that on the evening in question, the company director's car had remained on the driveway all night.

As a result of this double alibi, the man was eliminated from the enquiry, it being thought that the prostitute had got her facts wrong. However … .

On 6 May 1965, some ten months later, suspicion fell on the same individual when the same car was seen in the early hours in Kensington Church Street, and on this occasion the witness was one of the decoy patrols.

The company director was brought in just as swiftly as on the previous occasion. He denied being there and said that, whoever the person was, he must have been using an identical car with an identical registration plate. The prostitute was called to the station and upon seeing the car stated she was now more sure than ever that was the vehicle in which she had been the occupant; however, neither she nor the woman officer were able to identify the man as being the driver.

Fifty years later, I spoke to the woman officer involved for further details of the incident. 'Where did you get that load of rubbish from?' she demanded to know and, misunderstanding the question, denied ever working with a prostitute. In endeavouring to explain that I had not implied she and the prostitute were working in concert and what I had told her was a matter of record, I feared my explanation was not being accepted and therefore that matter should not be taken any further forward. After all, half a century to a nonagenarian's memory is quite a long time.

Matters were not helped by the prostitute now adding details to her original statement, inasmuch as there had been an argument over payment that resulted in her not being paid at all. It was beginning to look like a classic case of a prostitute 'getting her own back' by making false and damaging allegations against a client. Nor did it help that she had failed to report the 'attempted murder' to the patrolling police officer the same night as she walked home and in fact did not report it to the police until eleven days later. Further enquiries were made about her background that revealed her to be a notorious liar, and this was corroborated by her mother.

There was little doubt that the company director was the man in the car, on both occasions, but if the prostitute had got the day of their encounter wrong, his truthful alibi would strengthen his other denials. It was a highly unsatisfactory state of affairs but the matter could not be taken any further due, in part, to a story that had probably been embellished very foolishly.

Much more unsatisfactory than that was the dental surgeon. Aged forty-five, with two dental practices – he was also a Justice of the Peace – he came to the attention of the murder squad after a Ford Zodiac was seen on a number of occasions between 2 March and 29 April 1965 at Notting Hill Gate and Holland Park Avenue in circumstances that suggested strongly the driver was trying to pick up prostitutes. When the dentist was interviewed by DS David Hall on 10 May, he acknowledged driving the Zodiac, which was registered to his father. However, he said he could not remember being in those areas during the early hours of the morning, although he agreed that he might have been. He denied robustly being there to pick up prostitutes and said he had been going straight home after a conference. It was pointed out to him that he had been travelling in circles and his argument was weakened by the fact the women he had approached had been members of the decoy squad. Were these the denials of a highly placed member of the community wishing to save himself embarrassment? Quite possibly they were, and he was released.

Two months later, on 13 July he was interviewed again, this time by Du Rose, because it had been revealed that during the period 6 March–22 April, a Rolls-Royce had been seen on several occasions, in the same area and in the same circumstances, and this vehicle was registered to the dentist. He admitted the cars were driven by him and that probably he had been in those areas but staunchly denied being there for the purpose of acquiring the services of prostitutes. Finally, he rather pompously declared he did not wish to deny he was the person who had been seen by the decoy patrols.

It was clear that the dentist, a married man with children, merited a rather more searching examination than that, especially after he admitted owning a 12ft motor launch and a 90ft single screw motor launch, both of which were berthed at Sunbury. It was this latter vessel that the dentist admitted taking down the Thames with a number of people on board with the intention of putting out to sea but as they reached the Thames estuary they had had to return due to bad weather. This, he said, was during July 1964, the period when Mary Fleming had disappeared. It was fortunate that Du Rose was able to establish beyond doubt that the dates of this trip were between 6 and 10 July; the day before Fleming vanished. There was no record of the dentist putting either of his vessels through the Thames' locks during the period of the bodies of Tailford and Lockwood being found in the river.

Nevertheless, dust samples were taken from both cars and both boats, plus samples of vegetation from the vicinity of his home address. Laboratory analysis revealed they could not be connected with the murders.

However, the dentist had lied and lied to police. He had the opportunity to carry out the murders and the dental expertise to extract the dead women's teeth, but after making a great many other enquiries there was no evidence to prove he was the murderer.

***

As mentioned previously, from 15 March 1965, a number of women police officers were given the task of tracing missing prostitutes, and in addition anyone who had committed suicide who might be regarded as a suspect.

Between 20 January and 30 September 1965, nine men aged between 36 and 64 committed suicide by immersing themselves in the River Thames. None left suicide notes that would have been pertinent to a number of deceased prostitutes and one by one they were eliminated.

However, one who initially appeared to fit the bill was a Pole who, on 3 March 1965, three days before his 36th birthday committed suicide through an overdose of drugs. He left a note for his wife and family, telling them that he was, 'to blame for everything that happened'. Enquiries revealed he was a frequent visitor to clubs in the West End and also west London, where he associated with the prostitutes there and upon whom he spent a great deal of money.

However, he did not possess a car, nor could he drive one and his journeys to the West End were by means of taxis. These facts were verified by his wife, the club proprietors and his employers. The company that had employed him as an accountant for fourteen years carried out an audit that revealed serious discrepancies. He could not be connected in any way with any of the dead women and it was undoubtedly his financial difficulties that had resulted in the contents of the note that accompanied his suicide.

There was another man who committed suicide on the same day as the Pole; there was no connection between the two men but there was a link with the man and the Heron Trading Estate where he had been employed as a night-time security guard.

***

This 46-year-old man who lived with his wife and family in Putney committed suicide by inhaling exhaust fumes from his car in his garage, which was quite separate from his house and was, in fact, several streets away. He left a note for his wife that read as follows:

> I can't stick it any longer. It may be my fault but not all of it. I'm sorry Harry is a burden to you. Give my love to the kid.
>
> Farewell, Jock.
>
> P.S. To save you and the police looking for me I'll be in the garage.

So, what did this mean? Firstly, Harry was 'Jock's' brother. The first two sentences of the note could have been admissions to the murders but also they could well have referred to the fact that he and his wife had been on bad terms for some time; also that he was a heavy drinker. That morning, he had been due to attend Acton Magistrates' Court to answer a summons for failing to stop in his car when required to do so. This was the car in which he had committed suicide and its registration number had not been noted in any of the murder enquiries indices.

Would appearing in court on such a minor charge – the result, if guilty, would have inevitably resulted in a fine – been sufficient to push him over the edge? Not normally, although the reason why he had failed to stop might well be a contributory factor – and only he could answer that.

However, it was known that he associated with prostitutes on a regular basis via a family member who had close dealings with them. He had been employed as a night-duty patrolman from 6 October until 25 October 1964 and part of his duties involved visiting premises on the Heron Trading Estate. This covered the period when Frances Brown disappeared on 23 October, although he was not working on the date she vanished. Nothing was known of his movements that Friday night. A week before this, on 17 October, he was admitted to the Central Middlesex Hospital with minor head injuries after he had been found in the vicinity of Renaults Ltd on the Heron Estate. He said he had been attacked by two men but he had been drinking and the consensus of opinion was that he had sustained those injuries after falling over.

His next employment was with a cleaning company in Harlesden, NW10, which commenced on 13 November and three days after Brown's body was discovered he accepted a job as a cleaner with a company in Dundee.

On the date that O'Hara disappeared – 11 January 1965 – it was said that Jock was still working in Dundee. His contract terminated on 8 February 1965 and he arrived back in London on the day before O'Hara's body was believed to have been deposited at the Heron Estate.

It appears that no enquiries were made by police regarding Jock's employments prior to his work that took him onto the Heron Estate. His whereabouts at the times of the previous murders simply are not known. He could have been responsible for Brown's disappearance and murder but it seems that, according to the local police, he was firmly alibied in Dundee at the time of O'Hara's disappearance. If that was the case, it was pretty well a rock solid alibi; nowadays one can drive the 481 miles from London to Dundee in just over eight hours, using the M1–M6 link. However, that infrastructure was not fully completed in 1965 and the journey time would have been considerably longer. It is possible, of course, that Jock could have falsified his work records; it is similarly possible that the Dundee police were less than meticulous with their investigations.

His inquest took place just six days after his death. No one from the murder enquiry team attended and there is nothing to suggest they were aware of his demise. Instead, the police were represented by the local police constable who had been called to the scene. Having heard something of his domestic circumstances, the coroner had no hesitation in recording a verdict of suicide.

So there was certainly no direct evidence against Jock and whatever circumstantial evidence existed was very wobbly indeed. After all, the search of the Heron Trading Estate – and the enormous significance regarding where the bodies had been stored – would not commence until two months after Jock's death. It was then – and not before – that his name was brought into the system; it dovetailed with the fact he had been recorded as committing suicide since O'Hara's death by one of the women officers checking the missing prostitutes and suicides index. But although Jock was recorded as a suspect, little else was done. Both he and his wife possessed cars; neither of them were examined forensically. Nor was the house or the garage. Baldock did not particularly favour him as the murderer, no more than any of the other suspects and possibly a bit less. And neither did Du Rose.

Not right then, at any event.

THE COP

I t is obvious that Baldock fancied 'The Cop' as being the murderer; it is also clear there is not a shred of direct evidence that points to his guilt. But the circumstances surrounding this officer are bizarre.

Initially, the man had been a casual labourer but as soon as he had finished his National Service with the Royal Electrical and Mechanical Engineers, he joined the Metropolitan Police in 1956. He was posted to Fulham and Notting Hill as a police constable and later as an aid to CID.

Academically, he was quite sound, as befitted a former grammar school boy; he achieved respectable marks in his intermediate and then final probationary police examinations and passed the first-class civil service examination.

It was while he was studying to pass the examinations at the Detective Training School that there was an accident when he leant out of a sash window; the upper part fell down on his head, which rendered him unconscious and for which he received hospital treatment. His recovery was sufficient to enable him to later pass the CID junior course, which was a necessity to join the CID.

However, at a time when it was not necessary but certainly desirable to have been officially commended for meritorious work for inclusion into the CID, this it appeared had passed him by. In fact, his one and only minor commendation came the day after he was appointed to the CID.

Nevertheless, a CID officer he became in 1961, and he was posted to Kensington police station.

One officer (who left Kensington before the Cop did) recalled him: 'I thought he was on edge. He was never quite relaxed – a bit of a loner. I can't recall him being mates with anyone; he didn't get involved with the rest of the office. He was the sort of bloke that you could have a conversation with and then, half-an-hour later, you'd realise he'd never contributed anything to the conversation.'

It was clear that the Cop was not well liked. Odd things began to happen. Some court papers were set on fire. The Crime Book went missing and it was found in the street; the Cop would later admit he was responsible for the second of these peccadillos.

After less than a year at Kensington he was shifted within the division to Hammersmith police station in February 1962; one officer recalled a detective sergeant saying, 'This bloke's coming in under a cloud – let's not jump to conclusions, let's treat him sensibly.' If the personnel did behave in a compassionate way to the newcomer, it could be that those benevolent feelings were not reciprocated. Det. Supt Osborn later stated that he was not mixing with his colleagues in the way one might expect and that his work was 'careless'.

The Cop had failed the examination for detective sergeant the previous month but that appeared to be the least of his worries. He lasted at Hammersmith four months; a woman police officer's handbag was stolen and the suspect was chased and lost. No one could identify the perpetrator and the handbag was found, flung over a wall on to private property next to the police station, but suspicion hung over the Cop, who was dealt with for gross negligence and was transferred off the division, to Brentford police station, on 'T' Division.

Brentford has been described as being, 'depressed and depressing' and, covering an area of about 2 square miles, it was, in police parlance, 'a sleepy hollow'.

It was probably due to the torpor of the area that the lunatic gunman and double murderer Donald Hume decided to carry out an armed robbery at the town's branch of the Midland Bank in 1958. This was after Hume had been released from a sentence of twelve years' imprisonment for being an accessory after the fact to murder, having been acquitted of the main charge of murder. Knowing that then one could not be tried twice for the same crime, Hume presented himself at the offices of the *Sunday Pictorial* and confessed to the murder of which he'd been acquitted; the resultant 'exclusive' made him £2,000 better off. The money lasted him just two months; hence the robbery. Having shot a cashier, he made off with £2,000 and decided this was such a piece of cake, he repeated the exercise three months later at the same venue, this time acquiring a more modest £300. The townspeople (including the local constabulary) must have breathed a large sigh of relief when two months later, Hume was arrested, having murdered a local taxi driver following an armed robbery at the Gewerbebank, Zürich. This time he obtained some loose change and incarceration in the Regensdorf Penitentiary until 1976, when repatriation with his home country led to a term in Broadmoor Psychiatric Hospital, to bring home to him the inadvisability of shooting both British and Swiss citizens.

So it was to the lethargic Brentford police station that the Cop was transferred, the reasoning behind the move being that he couldn't get up to mischief there. At least, that was the idea; he did not get off to an auspicious start.

'I never had any dealings with him, but I never wished him well,' commented one former officer to me, who was on his CID course when he was informed that he would be transferred from Brentford to Hammersmith to make way for the partially disgraced Cop. It was a posting that was aggravated since the transferred officer was then living at Kew and would now have to endure the rather extended travelling to work.

Rather more nonplussed was the former aid to CID who carried out a tour of night-duty CID on 'T' Division with the Cop; in fact, he had accompanied him when he purchased the autocycle (a popular petrol-driven bicycle manufactured between 1902 and 1999) that would figure prominently in the astonishing events that followed. But the reason for the aid being bewildered was because the Cop mentioned the name John Reginald Halliday Christie and the address where he carried out his misdeeds – 10 Rillington Place. 'He said to me, "Ever been there?"' the former aid told me. 'When I said I hadn't, he drove us there, even though it was miles off our ground; I believe it was on Notting Hill's ground. If he said anything when we got there, I don't recall it. I was later interviewed by Chief Inspector (sic) Baldock and I mentioned this to him.'

Let's pause here, just for a moment. Christie's name has already been mentioned as having worked at Ultra Electronics at the Heron Trading Estate, the same estate where the bodies of the murdered prostitutes had been hidden. At the time of the nocturnal visit to Christie's former address, the name of the road had been changed to Ruston Close; it had been for the previous eight years, although the house where the murders took place was still inhabited and would be until the 1970s when the street was demolished.

This was the house, of course, where Christie had murdered eight women and then either secreted their bodies in the house or buried them in the garden; and when they were discovered a tobacco tin containing their pubic hair was found.

Is it therefore not odd that the Cop should drive through the night all the way from Brentford, through Chiswick, Hammersmith and Notting Hill – just to look at a house where a drooling pervert and a serial murderer of women once lived? And apart from it being a serious disciplinary offence to leave one's division while on duty, it was a foolhardy one, for an officer who, in the space of under four months had behaved in such a manner as to necessitate his senior officers twice transferring him.

Well, there you have it; I'm sure there's a charitable explanation for that type of behaviour, if one digs deep enough. There was also an explanation for the Cop's behaviour – by the Cop, himself – as to what happened next when, three months after his transfer, his career took a catastrophic turn. A security officer at the Admiralty Oil Research Laboratory, 931 Great West Road, Brentford saw an intruder on the roof who escaped down the fire escape, jumped on to an autocycle and made good his escape. However, the security officer jotted down the registration number and reported it to the police. Since the Cop was the only CID officer on duty at the time, he recorded the matter; the piece of paper that contained the registration number of the autocycle – which, incidentally, belonged to him – was found, torn up.

Upon being confronted with this allegation, the Cop denied culpability in the offence initially; however, when he was told he would be put up for identification as the attempted storebreaker, he admitted his guilt. An officer who was a probationary police constable at the time had been posted as both the communications officer and the gaoler; at a somnolent police station where many people had a great deal of spare time on their hands, a large number of practical jokes were perpetuated. During his short time at Brentford, the young officer had never known a prisoner to be detained, so when he checked the cells he was surprised to find the Cop occupying one of them. 'I thought someone had locked him in there as a practical joke, so I let him out,' he told me. His mistake was quickly pointed out to him and rectified. 'He was always very smartly dressed and quiet,' he recalled. 'Rather the odd man out.'

When he was pressed, the Cop admitted other more successful recent storebreakings in the vicinity. Of course, it is a grave betrayal of trust when a police officer breaks into premises but in this case, it was not so much the offence, which was serious enough – when Section 26(1) Larceny Act 1916 was placed on the statute books (which catered for these offences committed by the Cop) the maximum penalty was one of fourteen years' penal servitude – it was what was stolen that was peculiar.

When he broke into the Sycamore Woodworking Company, Commerce Road, Brentford, on 13 September, he stole nine paintbrushes, twelve files and £5 3s 0d cash. Two nights later, he broke into the Permutit Water Softener Company, also in Commerce Road, and as well as stealing £11 cash, he additionally lifted what was described as a 'King Dick' spanner. And on 15 September (or shortly thereafter) he broke into Coley Thermometers, London Road, Isleworth, where he stole 21lb of Virginia Tobacco, ½lb of Old Holborn tobacco and a packet of cigarettes.

He was charged, suspended immediately and within two months he appeared at the Old Bailey, where he pleaded guilty to these offences. The psychiatrist's report showed the Cop knew right from wrong but it was what was said in mitigation that was odd. These storebreaking offences, it was said, had been carried out to display his vindictiveness towards his colleagues in the Metropolitan Police. The Cop said he had been accused of matters at the various police stations of which he was innocent and it is quite possible he had not been responsible for all the extraordinary events that had occurred. But in the Cop's own words, 'My feeling, wrong as it was, was that if they thought so strongly that I was a black sheep, I will show them and *be* a black sheep.'

He had been a Metropolitan police officer for six years and thirty-eight days; now he was sentenced to a total of twelve months' imprisonment and, two days after his sentence, dismissed from the force with no pension. An eviction notice was served at the police married quarters where he had lived with his wife and child. He served just over seven months of his sentence and was released from prison on 3 July 1963. However, by March 1965, just two weeks after the O'Hara murder, Baldock received information that the Cop might well be responsible for the murders and that he was now a car salesman for a firm in west London.

How the information was received and from whom, is not known. It could have been one of Baldock's informants (no details of an informant's true identity were documented in those days) or a letter or telephone call from a member of the public. Quite obviously, it was someone who knew the Cop because the details of his occupation were correct. It might have been one of the Cop's former colleagues – in any event, everyone who had ever worked with him was questioned. Or, with his twisted psyche, it could have been the Cop himself. Whether he was culpable or not, it might have been his way of defying the police to catch him, as he had done previously during the spate of storebreakings. It would be as if he was saying, 'See if you can catch me!'

It might be that the suspicion was already there and whatever the source of the information, it could already have consolidated whatever thoughts Baldock possessed about the Cop. Eight months after the Cop's arrival at Kensington, Baldock also arrived on the division, following his promotion to detective chief inspector. There he remained whilst all the speculation about the Cop's behaviour was being aired and it was not until one month after the Cop's transfer to Brentford that Baldock, too was on the move, back to the Flying Squad; he had had seven months to make an assessment of the Cop's behaviour.

Whatever the case, Baldock got to work because, although there was no direct evidence against the Cop, the circumstantial evidence merited further investigation.

First, there were the spoils from his admitted storebreakings: insignificant items, paintbrushes, files and tobacco, as though they were tokens, just to show that he actually could break into premises and steal items, no matter how insignificant. There was the missing crime book and the other allegations, never proved, including the WPC's purloined handbag.

Then, look at the murders and examine the items that were missing there: all the victims' clothing, their jewellery, their teeth or dentures, their handbags – again, just tokens. At one stage it was suggested this was done by the murderer to delay identification but to what end? He must have known the victims would be identified by their fingerprints.

And second – and more disturbing – was that the Cop had worked in all the areas where the murdered women had last been seen or had been found: Figg, Notting Hill; Tailford, Hammersmith; Barthelemy, Brentford; Brown, Kensington; Fleming and O'Hara, Acton. It was at Acton where his police married quarters had been situated, not half a mile from the Heron Trading Estate.

Lockwood, who had been found at Chiswick, was the odd one out but it was quite possible she had gone into the water further upstream and had floated down the river to Chiswick. It was Kenneth Archibald who said he had pushed her body into the river at Chiswick but, of course, Archibald was a self-confessed liar.

Baldock had heard rumours the Cop had previously been seen climbing a tree to look at a woman in her bedroom – I, too had heard that, independently – and that he frequently went to Soho strip clubs.

Direct evidence against the cop? None at all. Suspicion? Most decidedly. And look at the words he used in his voluntary statement at the time of his arrest:

> When I broke into the premises I have mentioned, I did not set out to steal but rather to have the satisfaction of doing something which I knew my colleagues would have to work on, but get nowhere … .

Baldock got cracking. It was established quickly that the Cop had been employed by a car dealers company in the Old Brompton Road – this brought him back to the area of west London; and the Cop himself had moved to Essex, where he worked for a local branch of that company. He had been dismissed for inefficiency at the end of July 1964 but not before allegedly reporting sick on two days, with 'nervous debility' sometime in

July. It was on 14 July that Mary Fleming's body was found in Chiswick but despite the most searching enquiries at the company, no trace of the dates of this sickness could be found. This, in part, was corroborated by the Cop, who, one year later would say he could not recall reporting sick since leaving prison, something that was confirmed by his wife.

In the meantime, a meeting was held at Shepherd's Bush police station with ACC Gerald McArthur, the head of the newly-formed No. 5 Regional Crime Squad that covered the area of Essex, and a series of observations, both day and night, were carried out on the Cop, without producing any useful information.

In addition, enquiries were carried out to try to place him in the vicinity of clubs, pubs or the streets of west London during the material times, without success. In addition, the many cars he had used in the course of his business were checked in the various indices; none had been brought to notice.

The Cop became aware that enquiries were being made about him by the end of February 1965; he moved house and Baldock felt he had taken great pains that this should not be made known.

Eventually, he was interviewed at home in the presence of his wife, by Baldock and Du Rose. He stated that since his release from prison he had only been to London three times; on 23 and 30 October 1964 at the Motor Show, Earls Court, and on 25 January 1965, at the Washington Hotel, Curzon Street, W1, on a Volvo sales course.

On the first occasion, 23 October was the date that Frances Brown was seen to be getting into a car with a man, never to be seen alive again. On 30 October, it was another three weeks before Brown's body would be found; just half-a-mile away from Earls Court.

It was confirmed independently that the Cop was employed on the Volvo and Saab stands at the motor show, on both dates, finishing at 9 p.m. The victim, Brown, was last seen at 11 p.m. By that time, the Cop told the investigators, he was either home, or very nearly home, in Essex.

Enquiries were made to ascertain if anybody from either of the stands at the show – approximately 130 on each, plus other personnel – could recall having a conversation with the Cop, who saw him leave or left with him. These enquiries were never completed. The Cop stated he had gone to the

Motor Show by public transport on both occasions and had claimed the expenses from his firm. This story could not be faulted.

However, sometime in October 1964 – the precise date is unknown – the Cop was seen at Victoria Station by a former police colleague. This venue is some distance from Earls Court; although not to someone with a car. That is, if that was on one of the two dates on which the Cop stated he visited London, of course; but in any event, the Cop said he travelled to London by public transport.

Regarding the latter date, 25 January – it was on 11 January that Bridget O'Hara was last seen alive and 16 February when her body was found – the Cop's story of going to the Washington Hotel was verified, again by an independent witness and again he claimed expenses for travelling by public transport.

However, another former police colleague told Baldock of a chance meeting and a conversation with the Cop 'in the early part of 1965'. This was in the Fulham Road, outside Hereford Mansions; and that is a very long way from Curzon Street. Again, not to someone with a car; but if it was on the date that he went to the Washington Hotel, he had travelled by public transport. Hadn't he? It certainly appeared so; a witness was found who stated that he and the Cop left the Washington Hotel together and went to Liverpool Street station, where the witness caught a train to Chelmsford. The Cop stated that he had caught a train to Rayleigh, although the witness did not actually see him board the train.

I've no doubt that Baldock had the railway times checked; so did I, by consulting a 1960s timetable. This is what I came up with.

If the Cop left Earls Court at 9 p.m. to return home, he would have had to choose between taking the Piccadilly Line to Holborn and changing to the Central Line to go to Liverpool Street or taking an eastbound District Line train to Tower Hill and changing to a Circle Line train to Liverpool Street. Whatever route he decided upon, it would have taken him about forty minutes to arrive at Liverpool Street main line station. It would have enabled him to have caught the 9.44 p.m. train to Southend-on-Sea (Victoria), which would have arrived at Rayleigh at 10.39 p.m. From there to his home at Leigh-on-Sea, it would be quite easy to have arrived there by 11 p.m. if not before.

However, if the Cop had missed the 9.44 p.m. train, he could have caught the 10.18 p.m. train, which would have arrived at Rayleigh at 11.03 p.m.; and whatever means he used to travel to his home, be it on foot or by taxi, it is entirely feasible that he would have arrived home between 11.15–11.30 p.m.

And on 25 January, the same train times applied; and the Cop's companion who accompanied him to Liverpool Street main line station would have caught a train, direct to Chelmsford; he would not have been in a position to have seen the Cop board the train that would have conveyed him to Rayleigh. Therefore, taking all that into consideration, it seems certain that the Cop's account of his movements on those three days was a truthful one.

During Baldock and Du Rose's visit, the Cop said to his wife, 'They've come about what I mentioned the other month.'

His wife made a reference to his previous employers, to which he replied, 'Not that, the other business which we joked about.'

She exclaimed, 'Oh, not the nude murders?' and laughed. Both appeared completely relaxed about the interview.

And when it was discovered the Cop had advocated going to a cheaper panel beating and spraying company than the one usually used by his firm, this company was visited and dust and paint samples were gathered. Other similar companies in the area with whom it was thought he had contact were also visited and samples obtained. All revealed a negative result. And to negate matters further, Kim Taylor, who had compiled the identikit of the men whom she and Brown had met on the evening of 23 October, was shown a photographic album that included a photograph of the Cop. She failed to identify him.

Baldock felt personally that if the Cop was the murderer, he would certainly kill again, but nobody else was murdered and the enquiry could not be advanced any further.

In late September 1965, seven months after the discovery of O'Hara's body, the investigation was wound up. The large-scale maps, together with the car index plus other indices, the women police report and workbooks were inserted into the storeroom of the special constables' office at Shepherd's Bush police station where, using Key No. 9, they were locked away.

In the event that there was another murder in the series, they could be pulled out and used in the new system for the fresh murder investigation; but there wasn't, so they weren't.

THE ENQUIRY
WINDS DOWN

And so, it came to an end – the enquiry had not been completed but manpower had been stretched to breaking point to the detriment of other divisions when the Met was experiencing its worse crime figures ever and it had simply run out of money. At its peak, the enquiry had employed 213 police officers and had used seventy-one vehicles. Further assistance had been provided by the Flying Squad, Interpol, Thames Police, various county forces and Regional Crime Squads, based in the Metropolitan Police Area, Essex and Surrey.

If the enquiry had been allowed to run its course, would the murderer have been identified and arrested? No, probably not, not when one recalls the limited resources that were available to the police more than fifty years ago.

And forty years ago, matters were hardly any better. Donald Neilson went on the rampage between 1972 and 1975, carrying out a series of armed robberies in which three postmasters were murdered. Matters came to a head in 1975 when Neilson kidnapped, then murdered an heiress, Lesley Whittle. The press coverage (which nicknamed Neilson 'the Black Panther') was enormous and the investigation by the local police was spectacularly bungled. At that late stage, not only was Scotland Yard called in to oversee the investigation, but Commander John Morrison OBE, QPM was sent. It was the only time in the history of the Metropolitan Police that an officer of so high a rank was sent on a provincial enquiry. And yet, Neilson was arrested in December 1975, not as a result of four years' of enquiries but because a couple of beat coppers saw him in suspicious circumstances.

Were lessons learned? No, not really. The same year that Neilson was arrested, Peter Sutcliffe (dubbed 'the Yorkshire Ripper') began his murderous campaign with attacks on women (some, although not all, were prostitutes) and in his six-year reign of terror, murdered thirteen of them. There was a massive enquiry by three different police forces with three separate sets of files and indices and it was feared that when all the paperwork was housed in one building, the floors would not be able to sustain the weight. The enquiry resulted in 27,000 houses being searched and 150,000 people being interviewed; this included Sutcliffe – and estimates vary – between five and nine times.

Again, the murderer was caught in January 1981 after a check on the vehicle he was driving found it had been fitted with false plates; and West Yorkshire Police, who had been leading the enquiry, came in for ferocious criticism. It led to the introduction of the HOLMES (Home Office Large Major Enquiry System) computer, where the fed-in information can now be retrieved in a split second. In addition, the Police National Computer is now used where the registered keeper of a vehicle can be retrieved in the same amount of time and the complete list of Hillman Huskys, Commer Cobs or indeed any other make and model of vehicle would be made available in minutes, so matters are somewhat different. Add to that, radio communications have improved beyond all recognition, mobile phones, instant number plate recognition, CCTV cameras and, of course, DNA profiling. First discovered in 1953, it was not used in criminal cases until 1985. Put very briefly, the discovery of blood, saliva, hair or semen at a crime scene is able to place a suspect there.

And that being the case, in similar circumstances, with these up-to-date resources, would the murderer be identified beyond doubt and convicted, today? I feel sure that he would; and, what's more, the death toll would have been far less. So would the numbers of police personnel who were engaged on the enquiry. Still, this is now and that was then; and that was why on 3 July 1965 the night patrols were stood down, as were the women police patrols a day later. Three days after that, so were the women special constables.

The Husky Enquiries had already ceased on 30 May 1965 and the 'decoy patrols' had come to an end on 18 June. Although only half of the house-to-house enquiries had been completed, due to the chronic shortage of staff on divisions, this aspect of the investigation came to a halt on 28 August 1965.

It had been intended to make enquiries of the various armed services with a view to determining whether or not a serviceman was responsible; but this investigation was not even started.

It was suggested that detailed, expert dental examination should have been made of the victims' mouths. This facility could have been obtained from the Dental Estimates Board, Compton Place Road, Eastbourne, which had a team of experts ready and available to carry out these examinations. These, together with the pathologists' reports, could have proved invaluable but for some unaccountable reason, the Board was not asked to become involved.

Much of the ground covered early in the O'Hara investigation – indeed, as well as all the other investigations – should, as a matter of course have been looked at again, but with the sheer intensity and volume of the work, this was not carried out. Other important matters came to light during the course of the enquiries and they, in themselves, were not completed. This included enquiries made in the provinces; as the investigation came to a close, 180 provincial enquiries were still outstanding.

'I think with the high profile and the heavy press interest, Du Rose did a good job,' was David Parkinson's opinion. 'There weren't any more murders and we didn't have the forensic technology then.'

There was a final meeting of the officers; some attended, some did not. Those who did understandably have differing memories after fifty years regarding what was said, but rumours about the murder suspect started before, during and after that meeting and expanded in the years that followed.

'I felt the killings could be the work of more than one man,' wrote David Woodland.

'There was a rumour that the person responsible had embarrassing connections,' John Strachan told me, but firmly emphasised, 'but that was a rumour.'

Ken Bowerman said, 'We were later told that the No.1 suspect had committed suicide, just prior to him being arrested.'

'I did come away with the understanding that the suspect had died, so there would never be a suspect/prisoner arrested and brought to trial,' Janet Cheal told me, adding, 'I have always believed that.'

Rod Bellis was at the final briefing. He told me, 'As I recall, we were not given a reason but there was a rumour that the suspect had committed suicide.'

Also at that briefing was Malcolm Peacock, who recalled being told, 'Keep this to yourselves, the suspect is dead,' with the addendum, 'This information must never leave this room.' Police were obviously more trustworthy in those days, because Peacock told me, 'Believe this or not, I don't think I ever did tell anyone else about it.'

'I was at a meeting when we were told the enquiry was finished,' recalled Bryan Martin. 'There was a lot of discontent. One faction believed it was the garage owner.' (Which, quite conspicuously, it was not.) 'There was a strong rumour that an ex-officer who had left the force and had gone to Australia was involved; that he had died. There was a lot of controversy as it was thought the culprit had some knowledge of crime scenes and police procedure.'

Jeannette MacGeorge is unable to remember whether she attended the final briefing or not, but told me, 'All I do know is that ever since that murder squad, I have always known that suspicion had fallen on a police officer and that he had died.'

'I recall all of us being told that the squad was closing down,' recalled John Newman. 'We were told that not only had the location where the nude bodies were stored had been positively identified, the security man who had both the van and the keys to the premises committed suicide.'

Gerry O'Donoghue remembers being told, unofficially, that, 'The suspect was dead, having committed suicide but that he was a security officer.'

Bob Boyd was not at the meeting but, as he told me, 'As far as I'm concerned, it was rumoured that a night security guard was suspect for the murders. Apparently he jumped off one of the bridges over the Thames and died. I thought that they had searched his garage and forensics had been found that matched those found on the bodies of the victims.'

'It was months later that it was rumoured that the murderer committed suicide,' Geoff Cameron told me. 'He had been a security guard patrolling industrial sites in the areas we had been watching, in a company van. If true, perhaps the efforts of us on the night-duty squad had not been in vain.'

'There was one main suspect, a security guard by occupation,' said Bob Cook. 'At some stage he committed suicide. I cannot now recall whether he was ever brought in for questioning. There were various other suspects, but nothing ever came of them.'

Mo Darroch (Mo Dennison, as was) told me that a now deceased detective constable who had had dealings with a security guard at Acton, informed John Du Rose. The guard committed suicide but, as she told me, 'I'm convinced he was the prime suspect.'

Whatever was – or wasn't – said, Jane Rogers, who had been granted compassionate leave following the death of her father, returned to Shepherd's Bush after that final briefing. 'The whole enquiry was gone,' she told me, sadly. 'Desks, phones, everything.'

THE AFTERMATH

The 'tecs melted away. Jim Mitchell, who started off the investigations with the enquiry into the murder of Elizabeth Figg, was transferred to 'A' Division, right by the Houses of Parliament, but it was a short posting, lasting only four months. He had completed more than thirty years' service, his retirement lasted twenty years and he died just after his 75th birthday.

Soon after the conclusion of the Rees investigation, Fred Chadburn retired in August 1964. He had served for more than thirty-one-and-a-half years and he died almost exactly twenty-three years later. His co-investigator on that case, Jack Mannings, had several more postings (including running the Murder Squad) before being seconded to the Department of Education and Science for eighteen months. On the day he rejoined the force – 30 April 1969 – he also resigned. He had little option; he was now 60 years of age and had served for more than thirty-eight years. He had been awarded the Queen's Police Medal and had been commended on fifteen occasions. Much admired by the rank and file, Mannings became the first national security advisor to the National Museums and Galleries and later died, aged 85.

Bill Baldock remained on 'T' Division for another eighteen months before he was transferred to C1 Department at the Yard, but it was only seven months later that he retired, on New Year's Eve 1967. He had served almost thirty-one distinguished years and his retirement outdistanced his service; he lasted forty-seven years, harboured unpleasant thoughts about John Du Rose and died at the grand age of 97.

Like Baldock, Bill Marchant was similarly transferred to C1 Department. Two years later he was promoted to the rank of detective chief superintendent and six months after that, to the rank of CID commander, in charge of the Metropolitan Police's No 3 Area. It was there that he died in office, on 15 February 1973, of a coronary thrombosis. He was only 56 years of age and during his service, in excess of thirty-six years, he had been commended by the commissioner on twenty-one occasions. 'He was a wonderful man with a great sense of humour, using expressions I've never heard before or since,' recalled Peter Quested. 'We used to play snooker and if I potted a ball by means of a fluke, Bill would say, "That's like looking up a bull's arse for a calf!"' Baldock was a man's man, a dedicated working copper, and his demise was hugely mourned.

Two years later after the Lockwood investigation, Dick Chitty led the hunt for Harry Roberts for the triple murder of police officers and four years after that he was appointed one of the Yard's deputy assistant commissioners. In what I believe was one of his most perceptive decisions, he appointed me to the Criminal Investigation Department before retiring two months later. His retirement lasted only ten years.

Maurice Osborn retired one month after the arrival of John Du Rose on the enquiry; he died in 1988.

Ted Crabb ended his career on 'T' Division, which was where he had first commenced duty thirty years earlier; in fact, he served four tours on that division, totalling thirteen years of his service. He died just before his 73rd birthday.

Frank Ridge spent more than five years with the River Police and left in 1966 to spend the last three years of his service as detective inspector on 'W' Division, having served for just over thirty years.

Ken Oxford – he demanded haddock on the bone for his supper while on night-duty – was promoted to detective chief inspector and in 1969 became the assistant chief constable of Northumbria Police. Five years later, he was appointed deputy chief constable of Merseyside Police and in 1976, chief constable. A very hard-line senior officer, Oxford defended his men against scurrilous, politically backed allegations of misconduct and during the 1981 Toxteth riots deployed CS gas grenades and advocated driving vans and Land Rovers into the rioters. He was much admired by the rank and file, rather less so by the Labour-backed Police Committee. He was awarded the Queen's Police Medal, appointed CBE and knighted; he retired in 1989 and died aged 74.

Which left John Du Rose; his career went onwards and upwards.

★★★

Du Rose returned to the Yard, where he continued to supervise the detectives being sent out on major enquiries. *The People* had proclaimed 'his expensive bid to catch the murderer, a failure'. Just prior to Christmas 1965, there was a top-level meeting at the Yard, involving Du Rose, John Bliss, the commander of the CID, and Peter Brodie OBE, the assistant commissioner (crime). The assistant chief constable and co-ordinator of No. 5 Regional Crime Squad, Gerald Elwyn McArthur MBE, QPM had brought to their attention the activities of two brothers, Charlie and Eddie Richardson, and their gang, and what a horrifying story of barbaric torture it was. It led to a lengthy investigation and the trial and conviction of the gang for offences of robbery with violence, grievous bodily harm and demanding money with menaces, for which they received swingeing sentences. Charlie Richardson received the longest sentence: twenty-five years. Du Rose had not actually taken part in the investigation but, as the man in overall charge, the success rubbed off on him and did him and his career no harm at all.

On 30 March 1966, his place was taken on the Murder Squad by Jack Mannings and Du Rose was promoted to deputy commander of the CID; six months later, Det. Supt Leonard 'Nipper' Read, also newly promoted, reported directly to him after being told to smash the Kray brothers' empire.

The men appeared initially to work quite well together; Du Rose left Read to his own devices but when Read arrested a Kray associate, an American named Alan Bruce Cooper (he was known as ABC), and threatened to charge him with conspiracy to murder, he was flabbergasted when Cooper told him he had been Du Rose's informant for the past two years; something Du Rose admitted when Read confronted him. Read was absolutely furious at having been kept in the dark and, as he told me, 'I took him on to the stairs at Tintagel House and just let him have it.' (By that he meant a verbal broadside rather than a pugilistic one.) Cooper was a very clever, manipulative man who had also been an informant for the US Treasury Department, and Du Rose told Read that Cooper had not been run as an informant 'as such' and that they had not been in contact for some time. Had he put up any worthwhile information, said Du Rose, Read would have been the first to have heard of it, although this is something that Read still has difficulty as accepting as the unvarnished truth.

However, much of what Du Rose said could well have been true; he had no real idea of how to run informants and had failed to control Cooper properly. Therefore, it was left to Cooper to probably dominate and certainly use the relationship, and to put up Du Rose's name when the going got tough; it could hardly have got much tougher than being implicated in a conspiracy to murder with the brothers Kray.

Read salvaged the matter by taking very firm control indeed of ABC – and Du Rose, with an enigmatic smile on his face, went back to his cheroots.

Du Rose never expressed an opinion to Read on the identity of the nudes' murderer. 'Whenever I asked him about that (or any other case), he would simply nod and say, "Yes, I remember that one",' Nipper Read told me, adding, 'Let me say, I have worked with easier people!'

Promotion to Commander CID came to Du Rose on 1 April 1968; just over one month later the Kray brothers and their associates were duly rounded up on charges of murder and grievous bodily harm and in March 1969, they were sentenced to life imprisonment. Du Rose basked in the reflected praise, which was lavished (quite rightly) on Read and his team. Three months later, Du Rose's rank was regraded to that of deputy assistant commissioner, having been appointed OBE in the New Year Honours list. Nipper Read had to wait another six years before he was awarded the Queen's Police Medal for distinguished service; many thought his hands-on work merited a knighthood.

It was just about time to go; Du Rose had served almost thirty-eight and a half years but in addition, storm clouds were hovering over the Metropolitan Police. *The Times* enquiry was about to break, with tales of police corruption and of there being 'a firm within a firm' being splashed over the newspapers. And when Her Majesty's Inspector of Constabulary for Crime, Frank Williamson QPM (who hated the Met with a passion) was instructed by the Home Secretary to lead an investigation into the whole, sordid business, he and Du Rose clashed on the day of his arrival.

Du Rose resigned on 31 March 1970; Williamson took the opportunity to sneer that Du Rose 'had got the wind up' but the truth of the matter was that Du Rose had to go, on service. Sadly, his wife, Constance, had died in December 1968 from a painful disease; six weeks before retirement, he married Woman Detective Constable Merle May Taylor. Attached to the Flying Squad, she had been the first to volunteer for the decoy patrols and was much admired by her contemporaries. Aged 35, she had retired the year before Du Rose's resignation.

Du Rose became head of security for National Car Parks and (although it was said that he was going to live in Bournemouth) he retired to the Norfolk area. And then, things went rather wrong.

He decided to write his memoirs.

★★★

When many retired senior police officers decide to pen their memoirs they are often very selective about what they write. This is understandable; after all, who wants to read about their embarrassments and/or failures? Readers want to turn the pages of a book where, following one bit of dazzling detective work after another, the villain is unmasked, stammers out his confession and is properly brought to book for his crimes.

There are other reasons for retired 'tecs not wishing to include every facet of their investigations. Bert Wickstead was an enormously successful detective who was known as The Gangbuster; built like a tank, he roared through the underworld, causing the occupants a large amount of trepidation. When Barclays Bank in Ilford High Road was robbed of £237,736 in 1970, this represented Britain's biggest post-war bank robbery. Wickstead set to work with a will and a number of men were arrested, charged and convicted. However, when Derek Creighton Smalls (he was known to his fast-diminishing number of friends as 'Bertie'), who had participated in the raid, commenced his new-found career as a supergrass, he was able to name all the other participants in the robbery and was also able to say that Arthur Saunders, who had been sentenced to fifteen years' imprisonment for his alleged involvement, was not one of the gang at all. It resulted in Saunders being released from prison and when Wickstead wrote his rather dire memoirs, *Gangbuster*, he ensured that no mention of Saunders, the robbery, or indeed the bank, was made.

And when Ted Greeno, the two-fisted terror of the racetracks, who had been commended by the commissioner on eighty-six occasions, appointed MBE and retired with the rank of detective chief superintendent, wrote his memoirs, an astonishing number of villains all allegedly chorused identically upon their apprehension, 'Blimey, Guv'nor – you know everything!'

Probably one of the most forthright detectives to pen his memoirs was Jack Capstick. When the first 'Q' Car pulled out of Vine Street police station in 1933, so it was crewed by Capstick; he served several tours with the Flying Squad, led the post-war Ghost Squad and was a superb murder investigator. He introduced the reader to the liberal use of his truncheon, saying, 'I have hit quite a number of ruffians over the head, and they have gone over all right, but the best place to catch a man is right across the ear. That is the place I have always aimed for. It sounds brutal, I know (!)'

But returning to Du Rose, to be fair, he had had an enormously successful career. He was a household name and the newspapers (who had provided him with a catchy nickname) loved him because he inevitably provided good copy for them. He had a wealth of fascinating cases to insert into the book: Haigh, the acid bath murderer, the Messina vice-gang, the Richardson and Kray enquiries – all of them, names well-known to the public – as well as dozens of murders and murderers to discuss. However, the fly in the ointment was the conspicuous lack of success in the nude murders enquiries.

Let me make this clear; Du Rose had given this enquiry his very best shot. He had put all the resources he could muster into it but, in the end, not only had it not paid off, because the enquiry had of necessity to be run down due to the crippling costs it had incurred, plus the abrupt decrease in personnel, there were enquiries that were still outstanding. Could he have done any more? Not, perhaps, unless he had used the tactics used by a Machiavellian old detective chief superintendent, definitely of 'the old school', who told me of a similarly difficult to solve murder he had investigated around Kings Cross, many years before. About twenty suspects were put up; none of them admitted anything. So that cunning old copper, under cover of darkness, went to each of the suspects' addresses and posted an identically worded, unsigned note through each of their letter boxes. It read, 'The police are on to you – they know you did that murder! Get round to the police station quick and give them your side of the story!'

The following morning, four of the suspects presented themselves at Kings Cross police station to confess; at their subsequent trial, the matter of the notes received considerable airing and resulted in a tersely worded insertion in *Police Orders*, which read, 'The practice of sending anonymous communiqués to members of the public is to cease, immediately.'

Personally, I thought this was a pretty nifty idea but if it had occurred to Du Rose, it wasn't a concept he adopted – probably by then, he had too few troops for such an undertaking.

Could anyone else have done any better? Probably not. Jack Capstick and Ted Greeno were tremendous detectives, as well as excellent murder investigators with a whole string of successes. When Capstick hunted the murderer and rapist of a 3-year-old child in 1948, a fingerprint – not on file – held the clue to the killer. Capstick decided to fingerprint the whole of the 123,000 male population of the local town; three months later, fingerprint card No. 46,253 revealed the culprit. And when a girl was found dying after a brutal attack in 1945, her last words were that the person responsible was a British soldier. On the second day that Greeno had 300,000 soldiers confined to camp in order to fill in questionnaires, the war ended, making them eager to get out; but Greeno persevered and the soldier responsible had his death sentence commuted to life imprisonment.

Capstick and Greeno had retired in 1958 and 1959 respectively and although both of them had mustered huge numbers of officers in some of their investigations, it is unlikely they could have succeeded where Du Rose failed.

So when it came to writing his memoirs, Du Rose could hardly exclude this huge enquiry; since it had happened only six years previously, it was still fairly fresh in everybody's minds and if it were not mentioned the public (and almost certainly the press) would be in a strong position to demand an explanation: 'Why not?'

It would be humiliating to say, in effect, 'I couldn't solve the most talked about murders of prostitutes since Jack the Ripper' – and it would be no crumb of comfort to add that those murders committed in 1888 were not solved, either. Du Rose had also failed to arrest anyone for the murder of Countess Teresa Lubienska after a four-year enquiry when he was a detective chief inspector – coincidentally at Hammersmith – but at least that could be blamed on DCS Ted Greeno, who had died five years before the publication of Du Rose's memoirs and who had wisely omitted any reference to the Lubienska investigation in his own autobiography.

No. Nobody had been arrested and charged with the Stripper murders, that was for sure; but what about someone who couldn't be charged? Someone who, without a shadow of a doubt, was the murderer but was beyond the law? Someone who had perhaps fled to a foreign country where no extradition with the United Kingdom existed? Maybe someone who claimed diplomatic immunity? Perhaps someone who had been consigned to a secure mental hospital? But no. Those people could resurface to repudiate those scandalous claims and make Du Rose's memoirs a mockery. However, the fact remained that since the enquiry had folded, there hadn't been any more murders … .

The News of the World had tried to cheer up matters by referring to a diary the great 'tec allegedly pored over, a diary containing the names and addresses of all the likely suspects; but reassured its readers (and the suspects in the diary, provided, of course, that it ever existed) that Du Rose would, 'only ever disclose one name in the diary – and only if it can be proved that the man is the nudes killer.'

Now, there was a thought. What about someone who might well have been the murderer but couldn't answer back – someone who was dead? Who could fit the bill? Without actually naming him, it looked as though Jock, the late security guard on the Heron Trading Estate might be a suitable candidate.

★★★

In his memoirs, *Murder was my Business*, published by W.H. Allen in 1971, Du Rose was very canny. In the chapter dealing with the murders, he used the words, 'I know the identity of Jack the Stripper – but he cheated me of an arrest by committing suicide.' After detailing the investigation into the murders, he wrote, 'Within a month of the murder of Bridie O'Hara, the man I wanted to arrest took his own life … . We had done all we possibly could but faced with his death, no positive evidence was available to prove or disprove our belief that he was in fact the man we had been seeking. Because he was never arrested, or stood trial, he must be considered innocent and will therefore never be named.'

It was a clever move; some of what Du Rose had written was true (although not by any means the complete unvarnished truth) and the rest was not. The words floated in a kind of middle ground, a land of unsubstantiated myth. But – for the purposes of the book – he had demonstrated the fact this matter was unresolved was certainly not his fault; it was due entirely to the suspect, who had selfishly committed suicide. Had that not occurred, the reader was left in no doubt that Du Rose would have retired with his track record intact. In fact, Du Rose had gone out of his way to display fairness and impartiality; by refusing to name the suspect, he was displaying himself as being a scrupulously fair, decent, 'Dixon of Dock Green' type copper, so beloved by the British public. And when he said, 'no positive evidence was available', he was quite right. However, the media and the journalists put an entirely different slant on *that*.

RUMOUR AND
SPECULATION

In actual fact, Pennsylvania's *Reading Eagle* got in first when it decided to publish a two-page spread about the case on 30 April 1967. It is difficult to surmise why. Obviously it was written with an input by Du Rose but if journalistic licence wasn't readily used, then Du Rose was badly misquoted – or was he?

'With fingers crossed, Scotland Yard is unofficially closing its books on Jack the Stripper,' read the article. 'The Stripper's more than two year absence has led the Yard's top brass, including Detective Chief Superintendent John Du Rose, to the conclusion that this modern-day specialist in depravity murders may be dead.'

This may have been laying the trail for what would later feature in his book but what followed in the article was breathtaking in its stupidity. In describing the murderer's *modus operandi*, the article went on to say, 'In his paroxysms of lust, he not only strangled his willing sexual partners but beat them unmercifully about the face. In almost every case, the victim's breastbone was bruised.'

Of course, it was only Fleming who had sustained a heavy punch to her breastbone, and Barthelemy and possibly Tailford who had been punched in the face. But in a direct quote from Du Rose in respect of Elizabeth

Figg, 'She had been strangled and she bore the same facial markings and breastbone bruises as the Stripper's seven later victims.'

However, apart from that observation being incorrect, in his memoirs, Du Rose would completely discount Figg or Rees as being victims; as he would state, there were just the six victims, beginning with Tailford.

Du Rose was also quoted as saying, 'I don't hold with theories that he kept the women's clothing as fetishes in a black museum. I think he burnt everything. Furthermore, I don't think he actually stripped his victims. I think he offered them a high price to take off their clothes.'

Du Rose must have known that, with the exceptions of Figg, Tailford and Lockwood, hypostasis revealed that the five other victims *had* been stripped, after death.

The article concluded that for months the Yard continued its search, 'at a cost of $15,000 to $30,000 a week and used up thousands of police man-hours' until the Commissioner, Sir Joseph Simpson, reduced Du Rose's force drastically 'and sent him on a long-delayed vacation'. Again, Du Rose was laying the foundations for saying it was not his fault.

The People (who, four years earlier had described the investigation as 'a failure') was next with an 'exclusive' in November 1969, in which the killer was named as 'John X', an outwardly respectable family man, living in a London suburb. According to the report, a minute forensic inspection of this man's garage had revealed the paint deposits that had been found on the victims' bodies were also on the floor and on discovering that detectives had searched it, John X killed himself. What was more, his car registration number had been noted by police in the area patrolled by prostitutes and he had access to the factory estate where the bodies had been stored. So why had this not been reported by the police, to demonstrate that all their hard work had not paid off? Because of the 'fairness and humanity' imbued in the western world's finest police force, that's why – never to accuse a man unable to defend himself. They had accepted this case to be a 'failure' to protect the man's wife and children from the suspicion that he was 'the most insanely perverted sex killer of this century'.

Now, let's cut to the chase. Working upon the assumption that 'John X' was Jock, the security guard, this story was nonsense. Firstly, not only was Jock's garage never forensically examined, it was never even searched, not at any time. It goes beyond the bounds of common sense to believe that a crime scene, containing such a wealth of incriminating evidence, would be left to enable the lessee of the garage to return there, park his car inside it and then asphyxiate himself. Next, it would have been doubly difficult since, at the time of his suicide, the enquiry team were not aware of his existence. They were similarly not aware that the Heron Trading Estate had housed the bodies of the victims; it was only when they made enquiries there, months later, that they learned of Jock's existence. Ah, but what about Jock's car registration being noted by the night-time patrols? The simple answer is, it wasn't. Not at any time. And this noble desire to shield from his wife the notion that her husband was a killer? Nonsense. Following his suicide, plus the connection being made at the Heron Trading Estate, Jock's wife was interviewed at length about him by the murder squad detectives; and a great deal of pertinent information was forthcoming.

If that were not enough, there's another unconnected matter, full of similarities to Du Rose's case, which should be mentioned. Agnes Walsh, a prostitute who had just celebrated her 22nd birthday, was found dead in a boarding house in Paddington on 27 May 1950. She was naked, a handkerchief had been firmly thrust into the back of her throat and, in the opinion of the pathologist, a nylon that had been tied tightly round her throat had been placed there after death. It was discovered that her watch and two rings were missing and the investigation was taken up by DCI John Pretsell Jamieson. Tall, lean, hawk-faced Jamieson (he was known as 'Jock' and 'JJ') was a veteran of the First World War, the Flying Squad and the Ghost Squad; he would go on to be promoted to detective superintendent, be awarded twenty-nine commissioner's commendations and the Queen's Police Medal. Now, at 51 years of age, he began the hunt for Agnes Walsh's killer. Suspicion fell on a 29-year-old, quick-tempered man named Donald Davidson. The evidence against him was impressive but when Jamieson went to Davidson's home town of Houghton-le-Spring, County Durham, he was too late; Davidson had shot himself.

At Agnes Walsh's inquest, the coroner asked Jamieson, 'If you had come across Davidson and he had been alive, what would you have done?'

To this, Jamieson simply replied, 'I would have apprehended him and brought him back to London on a charge of murder'.

I mention this, because this is precisely what did *not* happen at O'Hara's inquest, which had been adjourned until 9 February 1966. O'Hara had already been buried for eight months when Hammersmith Coroners' Court heard evidence from the pathologist, Dr Bowen, and also Bill Baldock, who told the court that more than 120,000 people had been interviewed and that in excess of 4,000 statements had been taken. They did not hear from John Du Rose, to hear him say that had Jock lived – who, according to his memoirs, he had identified as the murderer, almost twelve months previously – he, like his contemporary, Jamieson would have 'apprehended him on a charge of murder'.

In fact, the coroner did not hear from Du Rose at all because he wasn't there, and therefore the jury returned a verdict of 'murder by person or persons unknown'.

When Du Rose was interviewed by investigative reporter Tom Mangold for the *24 Hours* programme, he alluded to a diminishing list of suspects, originally about twenty, and stated – without, of course naming him – that Jock was already a suspect. Stories were fed to the press along the lines that 'the net was closing in on the murderer' and that Jock was one of the final three names on the list but, before he could interview him, he had committed suicide.

If that were the case, it was rather at variance with a report in *The Times*, six months later. It bemoaned the fact that the murder squad had been run down, especially, 'at a time when the police are convinced that they are closer than ever to finding the murderer'. In fact, the article went a little further. When Du Rose was telling Tom Mangold that at the time of Jock's departure from this world, the number of suspects had been whittled down to three, six months later *The Times* was saying that the suspects were 'now fewer than six'.

Perhaps believing the account given to *The People* was a little too fantastic, Du Rose now leaked some information to *The Observer*, which described the suspect as a 45-year-old security guard but stressed that any evidence was 'purely circumstantial' and it was only after his suicide that his background was checked and that the result was, indeed, purely circumstantial.

In May 1971, the *Sunday Mirror* serialised Du Rose's memoirs and on 7 July the book was published; and there, for the time being, the matter rested.

★★★

It was clear that Bill Baldock was furious with Du Rose's disclosures; he did not accept for one moment that Jock was the killer and was certain he knew who was. It is also possible the journalist Owen Summers – he who had bestowed Du Rose with his charismatic nickname – was somewhat miffed at being knocked out of the bidding war for an exclusive with his protégé. And therefore it was not beyond the bounds of possibility that Baldock had a number of liquid lunchtime chats which, on 8 February 1972, resulted in Summers publishing a sensational series of articles in *The Sun*. The first, stretched over three pages, had the headline, 'Riddle of the Murdered Nudes' for the first two pages of the spread and this dealt with the first three victims plus Kenneth Archibald's strange confession. This was good copy by itself but the third page held the clincher, 'Was the Maniac Killer a Cop? And could he strike again?' In this part of the article, Summers debunked Du Rose's theories, one at a time. Yes, the security guard had been in Scotland at the time of one of the killings, and yes, he could have caught an overnight train to London, kill and return to Scotland. But, asked Summers, was it likely? Nothing was found in his car to link him with the killings, neither was any of the victims' missing possessions found in his home – of course, what Summers could not say was that neither car nor house was ever searched because that would have been pointing the finger at his source. But what he could and did say was there was no conclusive evidence linking the man with the paint markings found on the bodies of the women.

'Nevertheless, Du Rose, nicknamed 'Four Day Johnny' for the speed with which he cleared up murders, maintained that his theory was the answer to the riddle', said Summers. It was he who had created the legend of Four Day Johnny; now it appeared that the legend was going to be diminished as a myth.

So was the maniac a policeman? This was a possibility, wrote Summers, and added what he referred to as, 'a chilling fact' – 'Each of the women was dumped in a different police sub-division – invisible boundaries which very few members of the public would know.'

The readers of *The Sun*, with its daily circulation of more than 3½ million, could barely wait to see what revelations would occur in the next day's edition; in all probability, neither, I expect could Du Rose.

The 9 February edition of the newspaper centred on the last three victims (it being generally held until then that there had been six murdered women, rather than seven or eight) plus the forensic side of the investigation and ended with the final (and unbeknown to the vast majority of the readers, sardonic) paragraph, 'It was then that Scotland Yard put a mastermind in charge of the entire operation and set up a gigantic ambush that the killer could not possibly escape.'

'The Mammoth Ambush and the Men it Caught' was the headline for *The Sun*'s edition for 10 February and it detailed the enormous enquiry that Du Rose had launched. The men that it caught, however, referred to the kerb-crawlers who had been questioned. Owen Summers was leaving the best bit till last.

The 11 February edition's headline was 'Could this Killer Strike Again?' and in the final part of the series really hammered home the inconsistencies in Du Rose's story, so that if anyone had missed, or was in any doubt concerning Summers' grave reservations published three days previously, they wouldn't on this occasion.

No, Summers was in favour of Baldock's theory; that the killer was a cop and he presented it in the following format:

THE KILLER had a detailed knowledge of the alleyways and deserted places where the bodies were dumped. *A Policeman?*

THE KILLER must have somehow gained the confidence of the girls who entered his car thinking they would be safe with him. *A Policeman?*

THE KILLER was obviously a resourceful man who must have acted quickly and cleverly under personal stress particularly at times when perhaps minutes counted to avoid detection. *A Policeman?*

THE KILLER seemed to have been aware of the master-plan to check on every vehicle in the killing area. *A Policeman?*

Summers finished by hoping that Du Rose was right and that the suspect was dead. But, as he concluded, ' … after following the case, step by step, as it happened – and now again – I have come to the conclusion that he could well be alive.'

Well, that must have set *The Sun* readers' pulses racing – the thought that a prostitute-murdering maniac was still at large – but there was more to come. The headlines for the 17 February edition proved that, as they boasted, 'The Sun gets things done' because the headlines roared, 'Nude Murders: New CID Probe'. It is, of course, debatable whether or not DCS John Perkins of the Yard's Murder Squad did actually reopen the case (which had never been closed) or act on the file that Summers had allegedly sent him, since all the information was already contained in the Yard's file. Still, the newspaper took the opportunity to trash Du Rose's theory once more and added optimistically, 'Yard chiefs expect their latest inquiries to throw new light on several puzzling features of the case.'

★★★

Let us leave *The Sun*'s revelations for a moment and devote a little time to the subject of corrupt cops; because I knew a few of them. They were in the minority, I assure you – but they were there, all right.

I sought the arrest of a man for grievous bodily harm who for years had slipped through the net due to his ability to bribe police officers and intimidate witnesses. At the time, he was already on bail for a serious offence (this had cost him a £400 bribe) and when an informant set him up for a street ambush, I chose only absolutely trustworthy police officers to accompany me. Having arrested him, I walked into the CID office where another crooked cop was on the phone to the receiver of the £400 bribe. Looking straight at me, he said, 'Don't worry – that case won't be going anywhere.'

However, it did. Once my prisoner realised that I couldn't be frightened or bunged, he made a full confession and was kept in custody until he appeared at the Old Bailey and was sentenced to eighteen months' imprisonment.

The point I'm making is this. These officers behaved in that fashion because they knew they could get away with it. Who could I complain to? A very senior officer hated my guts; he was in the pocket of a certain east London criminal family upon whom I'd been leaning very heavily and felt it his duty to frighten me off; hair-raising times!

The downfall of this type of people came because too many of them were in the know; when crooked cops turned over a drugs dealer and helped themselves to his profits, they did so secure in the knowledge that their victim couldn't really complaint about their actions, given the provenance of the money they'd stolen. But other cops were present; and there were honest ones who didn't agree with the actions of the crooked few and who took the appropriate action to bring about their contemporaries' downfall.

Quite apart from a colossal arrogance – and that was the common denominator of all the bent cops that I've described – there was the necessity when the crunch came to cobble together a defence against these allegations. This meant they all had to agree upon a story and stick with it – and sometimes it worked and sometimes it didn't. But the crooked cops had an edge; they knew the way police investigations worked because they were seasoned investigators themselves.

However, for a rogue cop who worked alone, there was no need to confide in anybody, and as a consequence there was no risk of betrayal. Someone like DS Rodney Whitchelo, who in the late 1980s single-handedly ran a blackmail plot in which he demanded £4 million from the Heinz food company. He bought jars of baby food and spiked them with caustic acid and broken razor blades before returning them to the shelves. In one jar of Heinz cauliflower baby food alone there was sufficient poison in it to kill twenty-seven infants; it resulted in Heinz removing its brand of baby food, worth £30 million, from retailers' shelves.

Whitchelo achieved a small part of his aim; he obtained £32,000 from various cashpoints and because as a former Regional Crime Squad officer he was trained in the art of surveillance as well as police procedure, he was able to keep one step ahead of the 200 officers tasked to identify and arrest him.

He was arrested as the result of an investigation that cost £3 million and during his three-month trial at the Old Bailey, with customary arrogance, he claimed he had been set up by his former colleagues. In fact, 'evil and arrogant' were the words used to describe him by Her Honour Judge Nina Lowry when, in 1990, she sentenced him to seventeen years' imprisonment. Released after just nine years, Whitchelo told the press 'he wanted his victims to forgive him' including, presumably the 9-month-old baby who was rushed to hospital after consuming baby food laced with hundreds of razor blade shards.

So if Jack the Stripper was indeed a rogue cop, the investigators were at a distinct disadvantage. As I've said, the killer would be aware of the tactics used by his police contemporaries and would be also able to anticipate their next moves. And, of course, he was alone – there was no one he need confide in, nobody to betray him.

That is, if Summers and Baldock were correct in their assumptions, that the killer was a cop. Over to Du Rose; what did he make of these revelations?

★★★

Du Rose could not be expected to take this lying down and he didn't. In an article spread over two days, 21–22 November 1972 in the *Evening News*, the whole story was regurgitated; but there was no mention of a rogue policeman. There was no mention of a security guard, either; just the mention of the man whom Du Rose was about to arrest and who, within a month of Bridget O'Hara's murder, had killed himself, leaving behind the note containing the words (which were inaccurately recorded as), 'I can't go on.' This, asserted the newspaper, 'was Jack the Stripper.'

In Summers' series of articles he stated, 'In a report to his superiors, Du Rose claimed that this man (Jock) was the mass murderer; and that he committed suicide in fear of the intensifying police hunt.' Summers may have been employing a little journalistic licence and, oddly, this appeared to be backing up Du Rose's version of events. In any event, it was not true.

Baldock had prepared the report. Of course, Jock was mentioned as a suspect but purely because he had worked at the Heron Trading Estate at night and had been in the area where the women had been killed. He had associated with prostitutes but it appeared he was alibied for the time O'Hara was killed and nothing was known of his movements when Brown was murdered. It was certainly sufficient to place him in the 'suspects' category (along with twenty-five others) but he appeared no more culpable than anybody else with the exception of the cop, of whom Baldock stated:

> The circumstances surrounding his mental history, knowledge of the area and background are ideal in every respect for being the murderer. If he is the man responsible he will certainly kill again in the absence of any precautions.

Du Rose did not demur from these assertions. And far from stating that in his opinion the prime suspect was dead, when the file was passed to him for minuting, the following words are what he appended to the report dated 20 September 1965, which was forwarded to the Assistant Commissioner (Crime) through the Deputy Commander C1 and Deputy Commander Districts:

> I would only add and feel I must urge that despite shortage of staff, considera-tion be given to at least a few selected CID officers and/or aids being posted to special duties at night, if necessary for some considerable time, who, if unable to prevent another murder would at least provide some information in the event of a further death in this series.

It was Du Rose's polite way of saying, 'It wasn't my fault that the enquiry was run down and CID officers should be retained on night-duty because the murderer hasn't been caught and he's still out there.'

So the outcome of all Du Rose's carefully constructed bullshit for his book was this: the fact remained that despite Baldock's belief that the cop was the killer, he might well have been wrong and theoretically Jock still might have been the murderer; but it also meant that Du Rose's claims as to how the murderer was identified in his autobiography and in the media were nothing less than a disgrace; and an egotistical one at that.

What's the difference between a liar and a bullshitter? The Concise Oxford Dictionary does not define 'bullshit' – at least, my copy doesn't – so let me give you my own interpretation. A liar is someone who makes an untruthful statement in the hope that he'll get himself out of trouble. A bullshitter makes a statement, orally or in the written word, which he knows is untruthful. However, the difference between him and a liar is that the bullshitter has a complete contempt for his audience and his message is plain: 'You're such a bunch of mugs that you'll believe what I say'.

John Du Rose died, aged 69, on 28 June 1980. He had been one of the great detectives but this one major flaw meant that the man who was an idol to many police officers did indeed have feet of clay.

★★★

Two more years went by after Summers' revelations and now, in 1974, a Fleet Street hack named Brian McConnell wrote a book about the case, entitled, *Found Naked And Dead* which was also serialised – the racy sections at least, of which there were many – in *The News of the World*. Although it had been researched, both through old newspaper files and police contacts, it was written in a typical Fleet Street hagiographic style with the object of recounting sensational stories to readers of the red-top press. When it came to identifying the perpetrator, McConnell cobbled together a strange creature, named Big John, who appeared to be an amalgam of Jock and the Cop. Big John had apparently served in the Army during the Second World War where, in drink, he would beat up Italian women. Demobilised, he married, had children and joined the Police force. Repeatedly turned down for the CID, he left the force 'with a clean bill of health' and became a security guard, started drinking heavily and began his career of mayhem. His quest completed and satisfied that, having been denied becoming a detective, he had beaten his police contemporaries, he went into the kitchen and, in his wife's absence, gassed himself. 'I cannot go on', said his suicide note, leaving the police to wonder why his car had been seen in and around the prostitutes' beats, on so many occasions. So that, together with a string of ludicrously made-up conversations between the murdered prostitutes and their clients, was McConnell's contribution.

It was just one of a number of preposterous stories that began to emerge about the nudes murders. One had DCS Ted Greeno investigating the murders right up until the time that Du Rose took over in 1965. A little research would have revealed that Greeno had retired five-and-a-half years earlier. Another had Jock, ten years younger than he actually was and living north, instead of south of the River Thames, committing suicide and a keen-eyed detective making a telephone call to the Yard. Within an hour, Du Rose had told Commander Hatherill (who had retired five months previously) that the nudes' murders were solved but that they should make no announcement about it – just to wind the investigation down. Since he wasn't there, Hatherill would have had pronounced difficulties in agreeing that imbecilic course of action but that – according to this very odd story – is just what happened; the enquiry was wound down seven months later, having incurred thousands of more man-hours and hundreds of thousands of pounds in expenditure, just for fun, at a time when the Met was experiencing the worst crime figures ever.

Everything printed about this unfortunate enquiry was descending into complete and consummate bollocks, but more was to come.

HANS CHRISTIAN ANDERSEN AND CO.

Welcome on board the good ship *Bullshit*; we're about to cast off on a journey to Fantasy Island, to enjoy a veritable feast of fairy stories.

It is inevitable in an unresolved enquiry such as this that there will always be someone, usually entirely unconnected with the case, who comes up with a prime suspect. It is not necessary for there to be one speck of evidence attached to this revelation, just a few items of similar information, no matter how obscure. It is necessary, from a legal point of view for that suspect to be dead, of course, and a bonus for him to have been well known. In the meantime, the provider of this information can pontificate to his heart's content and bask in the adoration of the simple souls who believe this nonsense; and should it later be proved beyond doubt that this person's prime suspect could not have been the culprit, he has two choices of action. He can (a) arrogantly state that no matter what anybody else says, he's right or (b) can climb down from his perch and mutter in a hurt sort of voice, 'Well, I did say it was only a rumour.'

One such alleged suspect was the boxer and media personality, Freddie Mills. 'A very interesting subject,' Michael Nesbitt told me. 'I know "Nosher" Powell said Freddie Mills was supposed to be the one that was doing the murders but he said he didn't believe that and said it was a rumour started by 'the Soho Don', Billy Howard ...' (as indeed it was). So Freddie Mills is as good as anybody to start off with, together with a couple of other nonsensical subjects to be identified as Jack the Stripper.

From the early 1970s onwards, rumours grew that Mills was Jack the Stripper and as the flames of gossip were fanned, so the supposition became a certainty. Surprisingly, some police officers spread the rumours. One excitedly imparted the news to his fellows that a Scotland Yard detective had told him Mills was 'definitely' the killer. Another, from a far-flung constabulary, told a less convincing story that he had been to the Yard, had seen the Stripper file and contained in it was a suicide note from Mills, confessing to the murders.

Freddie Mills was born in 1919 and learned his trade as a boxer in the hardest school of all, fairground boxing booths, where he would often have half a dozen fights in one evening. He earned the nickname 'Fearless Freddie' and idolised the former American heavyweight champion, Jack Dempsey, 'The Manassa Mauler'; it was suggested that if the referee had said, 'Jack, the other fellow wants to fight with these double-bitted woodman's axes instead of gloves', Dempsey would have replied, 'Right. Give me one of 'em and get the hell out of the way!'

Mills was very much in that mould, a really gutsy, two-fisted fighter who would sometimes take two or three punches to land a good one of his own. At 5ft 10in, weighing 12st 6lb, Mills had ninety-six bouts, winning seventy-three of them, and took the world, British, European and Empire light-heavyweight titles. Perhaps unwisely, he stepped into the heavyweight division but, as Fearless Freddie recalled, in his days as a fairground boxer, he had got into the ring with opponents who were 2st, sometimes 3st, heavier than him.

Mills had held the world light-heavyweight championship for eighteen months before his last fight in 1950 against the American Joey Maxim who, with a left-right combination, knocked him out in the tenth round. You could beat Mills but you couldn't make a loser out of him. He capitalised on Maxim smashing out three of his teeth by cashing in on the popular song of the day, *All I Want for Christmas is My Two Front Teeth*, invested his career's £80,000 winnings in a restaurant and nightclub, and appeared on television, radio and in eight films. He raised funds for disadvantaged people and formed the Freddie Mills Boxing Club in Camberwell, south London. In the same way that his hero, Dempsey, was fêted by the American public, both during his career and in retirement, so the British public adored Mills.

Mills was found dead from a gunshot wound in his car on 24 July 1965. His club appeared to be in financial difficulties and he was said to be depressed. The weapon, a rifle from a shooting gallery, had been borrowed, by Mills from a friend. A police investigation concluded it was suicide and that was the conclusion reached at the inquest. However, although his wife, Chrissie, also initially agreed with the suicide verdict, she later changed her mind and asked the three-time winner of the Lafone boxing trophy, Det. Supt 'Nipper' Read, who was then investigating the activities of the Kray brothers, to make further enquiries.

However, after making the most searching investigation, Read came to the unhappy conclusion that Mills had indeed taken his own life. Chrissie Mills was furious with that deduction but, as Nipper told me fifty years later, 'Mills' daughter, Susan, said to me that despite everything that had been said about her father, "he was my dad".'

And a great many unsavoury things had indeed been said about Mills; that he had been in debt to, and threatened by gangsters, his suicide had been staged by Chinese gangsters who wanted to take over his club – his partner was Chinese – that he had been arrested for indecency in a public toilet and that he had homosexual relationships with the popular singer, Michael Holliday (who had also committed suicide) and also Ronnie Kray (who later denied it). More, however, was to come.

Following the sensational arrest of a number of Scotland Yard detectives who were jailed for corruption in 1977, of whom the highest ranking officer was Commander Wally Virgo QPM (he was later cleared on appeal), it was discovered that as a detective chief inspector at West End Central in 1965, Virgo had headed the enquiry into Mills' death. Furthermore, he had been assisted in the investigation by DS Gordon Harris who, in 1972, was convicted of corruption and sentenced to six years' imprisonment – and that investigation had been headed by DCS Bill Moody who, in turn, would stand in the dock with Virgo, five years later and, like Virgo, be sentenced to twelve years' imprisonment. It was the sort of melting pot that conspiracy theorists dream about – officers were found guilty of corruption; therefore, their conclusions on Mills' death must also be questionable. The debate as to whether Mills committed suicide or was murdered will, I suspect, run and run.

If that were not enough, the idea was propagated that because Mills was a boxer and because most of the victims had teeth knocked out – and, of course, he had allegedly committed suicide after the last murder – *voila!* He *must* be Jack the Stripper.

In 2001, Tony Thompson, the crime correspondent for *The Guardian*, reported that 'reformed south London gangster, Jimmy Tippet' had interviewed three generations of criminals and boxers to point the finger at Mills for a forthcoming book. Fifteen years later, we're still waiting for it.

So let me pre-empt the south London octogenarian pugs and thugs, who knowingly tap the side of their nose with one grubby forefinger, wink and portentously murmur, 'Yer. One 'er these days, the truth's gonna come out about Freddie Mills,' because I can save them the trouble, at least as far as the Nude Murders are concerned.

There is absolutely nothing, not one shred of evidence, to connect Mills with any of the murders and he was never considered a suspect by any of the enquiry team. If that's Fearless Freddie out of the frame, we can proceed to the next so-called suspect.

★★★

The suspect I refer to is not Jimmy Evans; he wrote an often unintentionally hilarious biography entitled *The Survivor.* The kindest comment that can be made about the book is that Mr Evans possesses a very lively imagination.

His contender for Jack the Stripper is a man he never met, namely DCS Tommy Butler, the head of the Flying Squad.

Just for the record, a quick look at Butler. Born in 1912, Thomas Marius Joseph Butler joined the Metropolitan Police in 1934 and in a glittering thirty-four year career, this highly respected detective served on the Flying Squad for seventeen years. A workaholic who often worked sixteen-hour days, he successfully cracked the Great Train Robbery, was commended on thirty-five occasions and was appointed MBE.

Because Butler was unmarried, lived with his widowed mother in Hammersmith and arrived home late at night – and more importantly, since Butler died of cancer in 1970 – Evans has managed, on no evidence whatsoever, to cobble together a set of circumstances where it can be inferred that Butler was a sexually repressed pervert who released his sexual urges by using prostitutes and then, suffused by guilt, strangled them.

Still, if you want to accept the word of a self-confessed perjurer who uses the phrase, 'On my daughter's deathbed' in an effort to establish his veracity, then Butler's your man. If not, it's time to pass straight on to the final outsider.

★★★

Harold Kenneth Jones was just 15 years of age in 1921 when he attempted to rape and then strangled 8-year-old Freda Burnell in Abertillery, Monmouthshire. He was arrested and, at Monmouth Assizes, he was acquitted. Just two weeks later, he cut the throat of Florence Irene Little, aged 11, and secreted her body in the loft of his parents' home. Arrested once more (and again, loudly protesting his innocence) he again appeared at Monmouth Assizes. But now, in a surprise statement, not only did he admit murdering Florence Little, he also admitted the murder of Freda Burnell. He was getting perilously close to his 16th birthday and, thanks to the provisions of the Children Act 1908 that banned the execution of juveniles under the age of 16, he was detained at His Majesty's Pleasure and served twenty years' incarceration.

Some time after his release he moved to London and in 1948 at Fulham he married, using the alias of Harry Stevens, and he remained living in Fulham until 1962. It appears he lived in the Putney area until 1965 when, following the last of the murders, he changed his name back to Jones and moved into a house in Hammersmith. There he remained until his death in 1971.

The highly questionable relevance of all this is that his last address was quite close to the addresses where two of the murder victims had once lived – and who by then were dead – and his address in Fulham had been near to a third – when she was alive. He additionally lived at an address three junctions away from Jock's garage prior to his suicide and another address, also three junctions away in a different direction, after Jock's death. Of course, so did hundreds upon hundreds of other men.

On the basis of this – together with some rather odd references to passages from the Bible – Neil Milkins in his book, *Who was Jack the Stripper?* invites the readers to believe that Jones was the murderer. The book is extremely well researched into the murders and Mr Milkins has contacted many of the relations of the victims as well as Jones' family; but truly believing (as Mr Milkins quite obviously does) that someone has committed an offence, does not make them guilty and despite filling the pages with supposition, bold type and exclamation marks, there is not one scintilla of evidence to show that Jones was the murderer.

★★★

Needless to say, none of the above-mentioned 'suspects' were ever considered by the murder squad; their names were never mentioned.

It's precisely this type of hypothesising – where according to the originator, the suspect *must* be guilty – that finds a parallel in fictional television crime series of which the now defunct *New Tricks* and *The Bill* were often the worst offenders.

The viewers would be in little doubt regarding the guilt of the offender, who would duly be arrested. There would be some fairly sharp police questioning, which would cause the prisoner to gulp before steadfastly replying, 'I ain't saying nuffink more until my brief gets here.'

Well, that's it, isn't it? Nothing else could be more incriminating than the guilty look on the suspect's face and those words which, to the viewers, would be a clear admission of guilt, where not one jot of evidence existed before. It would be sufficient for the arresting officers to give each other a self-satisfied smirk before heading off to the pub (the paperwork could of course, be completed another day) for a congratulatory drink, leaving the credits to roll and the theme music to play, heralding the conclusion of another episode and one more well-solved case.

Except, of course, life's not like that. Detectives do not appear in the witness box at the Old Bailey and say, 'So when the defendant said, "I ain't saying nuffink more until my brief gets here", this was a clear indication of guilt, my Lord and I therefore charged him with the offence and my colleagues and I went off to the pub and got pissed.'

To convict a guilty person, it requires just a *soupçon* more than the fartfull of fantasy dreamed up by television writers; and sometimes, that's not enough, either.

Let me give you an example. More than forty years ago, I was a junior CID officer attached to a murder enquiry. Someone had broken into a disused shop and set fire to it; a man who lived in the upstairs flat and who was asleep at the time, died as a result of smoke inhalation. A suspect came into the frame; he was questioned and denied any culpability in any way with the offence. When his clothing was taken as evidence, it was noticed that he had a quite a number of fresh scratches on his back; his explanation for these marks was scarcely credible. His back was photographed and then the chief inspector in charge of the case revisited the scene. Access had been gained to the shop via a smashed window; jagged glass was still apparent in the window frame. So he had the complete frame carefully removed and then had the carcass of a pig dragged through it. The striations on the pig's body matched those marks on the suspect's back exactly, and he was charged. I'd say that was compelling evidence, wouldn't you? Even better than fingerprints? Not so far as the criminal justice system was concerned; the case was thrown out at the magistrates' court due to lack of evidence.

So when the strongest possible evidence, such as that, isn't relied upon, you can perhaps appreciate my exasperation when the guilt of a man is implied because he happened to move to an address quite close to where two murder victims once lived.

So who's next? Ted Heath? Ronnie Kray? They didn't like women, did they? Both dead, aren't they? Well, stands to reason one of 'em must be guilty, don't it?

May God protect me from all amateur sleuths.

COLD CASE

David Seabrook's book *Jack of Jumps* was published, which was an account of the murders. In it, he claimed he had access to the police files in the case and there is no doubt that he did. He also named the person at the National Archives who allegedly permitted this disclosure, a claim denied angrily by the person concerned.

Seabrook stated the research took him four years to accumulate and, it is true, contained in his book is a wealth of information regarding the murders. Unfortunately, he chose to write it in a revolting, misogynistic, pseudo-tough guy style that often makes little sense and where the victims are referred to in a disgusting way. Everybody else is described in a sneering, contemptuous way – the plucky women police decoy patrols are offensively dismissed as 'law whores' – and the detectives are jeered at for their lack of success.

What the deeply unpleasant Mr Seabrook (who died aged 48, apparently from a heart attack on 18 January 2009) does do is to point the finger of suspicion at The Cop. So much so that he sent an 'Intel' (Intelligence) Report to Essex Police in 2006. This was following a BBC *Look East* programme that had a slot on an Essex cold case review team, so no doubt this was an act to whip up publicity for his book that had been published on 1 May 2006. This being a Metropolitan Police investigation, Essex Police passed it on to Scotland Yard's Specialist Crime Review Group, where it arrived on 8 August 2006.

The team extracted all eight files on the murders and sifted through them laboriously. The review was finally concluded on 20 May 2007 and came to the conclusion that, although there were similarities in the case of Elizabeth Figg with the last six murders, her murder was thought not to be part of the series. This was in contradiction to Baldock's theory that she 'could well' have been the first of the murder series. Gwynneth Rees was similarly dropped out of the loop. Of all the still living suspects, none were interviewed. Obviously, it was felt that the maximum amount of information that could be extracted from them had been carried out at the time. The reviewers felt that, of all the named suspects, many pointers indicated that Jock was the killer.

However, there was one matter that could not have been covered at the time of the original investigation. If DNA profiling had then been in existence, this would have settled the matter one way or the other; DNA samples would have been obtained from all the subjects and compared with the semen found on the victims' vaginal and throat swabs, which would have confirmed the guilt or innocence of the person concerned – simple.

Therefore all that needed to be done in the review to resolve the matter was to request those suspects still living to supply a DNA sample – a mouth swab would be sufficient – and if Jock was still such a strong suspect, to exhume his body from Putney Vale cemetery where he now reposes and that would bring the matter to a satisfactory conclusion. However, there was just one problem.

Of the slides containing the samples of semen taken from the corpses, there was no trace. In fact, no exhibits, pertinent to the case – and despite the most extensive search by the review team – could be found.

★★★

This is the moment when the conspiracy theorists will have a field day; hugging themselves deliriously, they'll believe willingly the disappearance of the scientific exhibits are on the doubtful lines of the JFK assassination and the Roswell UFO incident.

In fact, it's nothing of the kind.

The Home Office Forensic Science Service (FSS) took over the running of the Forensic Science Laboratory at Lambeth and other sites on 1 April 1991. Very much like the National Criminal Intelligence Service (NCIS) – also run by the Home Office – that opened exactly one year later, it was an unmitigated disaster. NCIS was disbanded in 2006 and the FSS closed four years later.

During the tenure of the FSS there were grave concerns that many old case files (some containing slides) would be lost and this proved to be the case.

Exhibits from historical cases were to be found in the unlikeliest of places. The noted crime scene investigator, Paul Millen, recalled that when he was working in Surrey, a cold case where the original investigators had long since retired was only solved after the original exhibits were discovered, by luck, in the corner of a storeroom in a police station, thirty years after the offence.

It could well be that similar exhibits have been stashed away in other police stations, but with the speed with which the various police services (especially the Metropolitan Police) are selling off police stations and other police buildings, if anything of any relevance is ever found, it will probably be by the Middle Eastern owners who are eager to transform those once-proud buildings into luxury flats.

So what are the chances of bringing Jack the Stripper to book for his crimes – if he's still alive, that is? Pretty slim, I'd say. Yes, one day those missing exhibits might actually turn up in the unlikeliest of police premises, and if that's the case the DNA could be compared with that of the suspects, dead or alive. It could be, of course, that the killer might be someone not mentioned on that list; therefore the entire DNA database could be checked but if the killer had led an otherwise blameless life, then he might never be identified.

However, even if those missing exhibits were to be uncovered, who would present them? Would there be a break in the continuity? It would only take one person to be unavailable in the sequence of exhibits being passed from one person to another for the defence lawyers to have a field day. And what about the suggestion of the evidence being contaminated? This is always a favourite with the legal profession. Who would give evidence? All the senior investigating officers are now dead. The former officers that I spoke to all served in a subordinate capacity. And the other witnesses – dead? Missing? Making themselves deliberately unavailable?

Well then, what about a confession? Given the case of Kenneth Archibald, who falsely confessed to the murder of Irene Lockwood, the Crown Prosecution Service would tread even more warily than they do now. If the confession was not backed up by any corroborative evidence, I should be most surprised if the person concerned ever made it to court; and the same applies to a suspect being fingered for the crime by a third party.

There's perhaps one other way.

Ever been a party to a house clearance? If not, don't volunteer for one; I have, and it's a miserable, melancholic experience. But just consider this scenario. A person vacates a premises, either because he's died or moved elsewhere. The new occupier moves in and discovers that the property has not been cleared as scrupulously as one would wish for. Because in the shed, the loft, the eves, wherever – there's an old traveller's trunk of the type you see in black and white 1930s films, the sort that would bear stickers displaying, 'Hotel George V, Paris' or 'Grand Hotel Excelsior, Venice'.

And when the chest is opened, it emits a musty smell; it is full of women's clothing. There might be a high-necked black jumper – just like Helene Barthelemy was wearing the last time she was seen alive. Perhaps a red suspender belt, of the type favoured by Mary Fleming. And there might be something else; a container, perhaps an old tobacco or coffee tin that rattles when it's picked up. Inside are an assortment of teeth, and perhaps a couple of sets of dentures.

If that were the case – and if the new occupier didn't take them down the local refuse tip but brought them to the attention of the police who thought them worthy of further investigation – the former householder might well have some tricky questions to answer.

It's a thought though, isn't it?

★★★

When my publishers first asked me to write this book, they caught me on the back foot. I was waiting for my next, *The Wrong Man*, to be published and I'd approached them with three different scenarios, any one of which I thought, would make a splendid book. But no – all of them, rather contemptuously, I thought, were peremptorily dismissed and I was told quite unequivocally that what they wanted from me was a book about Jack the Stripper.

I was nonplussed; I told them, I had no knowledge of the case, I knew no one who'd featured in it and, what was more, from the little I'd heard about the investigation, it was pretty seedy. All of the victims were prostitutes, no one had been caught for the murders – I was dimly aware that a security guard who had committed suicide had been favoured for it – and I knew that one or two other books had been written about it. Ah, I was told, but the same applied about Jack the Ripper – victims all prostitutes, killer never caught – and look how many books had been written about him and, in fact, were still being written? Finally, they appealed to my vanity; as well as being an author, I was reminded (if indeed I needed reminding) that I was once a Scotland Yard detective – who better to write an account of the Stripper than one who had been involved in large scale investigations?

Actually, they did have a point. I'd been involved in the murder investigation of a Soho prostitute and her maid who had fallen foul of The Maltese Syndicate and I'd encountered prostitutes during the course of my duties, both at home and abroad. I was advancing through the darkness of De Wallen district of Amsterdam towards the adjoining area of Chinatown to carry out raids on Triad premises during the 1970s when I felt I was being watched. Looking round, a naked and rather bored looking prostitute was observing me behind the glass of a shop window. She displayed no enthusiasm about continuing our brief eye contact meeting and with my companions urging me to hurry up, I was rather glad to proceed to the drugs bust.

The bevy of absolutely drop-dead gorgeous naked blondes I encountered in a club off Berlin's Kurfürstendamm were a sight to behold – I thought they were exotic dancers, but no, they were all toms. As my Bundeskriminalamt (German Federal Police) colleague worriedly pointed out, 'Remember, Herr Kirby, if anybody asks you tomorrow, we were visiting the Gemäldgalerie.' I agreed solemnly that this would be the wisest course of action, although I thought it rather unlikely that any fiercely moralistic disciplinarian would accept that an art gallery might be open at midnight.

Even more unlikely was the middle-aged lady I met on the Lyon to Paris express, en route for an away-day for shopping in the City of Lights. During the two-hour journey, she informed me that she earned a supplement to the housekeeping by soliciting on the train, and although I had no hesitation in diplomatically refusing her blandishments, this, she told me was a rather good wheeze used by many bored Lyon housewives for a little pocket money. So the journey passed with the lady grandly informing me of her visits to milliners along the Rue de la Paix and of sumptuous luncheons when she consumed posh tuck in the Tour d'Argent, although I did think the accuracy of these statements was on a par with my art gallery alibi. I left her at the Gare de Lyon, hoping that during the return journey she would be sporting a '*charmant* leedle 'at, *non?*' and a willing, panting customer.

So I suppose I was as well-placed as anybody to write such a book, but as I warned my publishers, 'Don't expect me to be able to pull the Stripper, like a rabbit, out of a hat.' I have to admit though, I did say this with a certain amount of self-deprecation; after all, hadn't I had my successes as a Scotland Yard detective? How splendid it would be if, having completed the typescript, I could stroll into the publisher's office, dump the 250 or so pages casually on the desk where, amidst their cries of delight, I could nonchalantly murmur, 'Oh, by the way, that's the Jack the Stripper case solved – what d'you want me to write next?'

What a conceited thought; to think that I could succeed where the likes of Du Rose, Baldock and Osborn had not. All I could do was to trail in their footsteps and marvel at the tremendous effort and man hours they had put into the enquiry; I spoke to their contemporaries but none could put the finger on the killer.

So what it comes down to, is this. I can't name Jack the Stripper because I do not know who he is. Remember what I said in the prologue to this book about not having any preconceived ideas about a person's guilt – and remember how wrong I was about the identity of the culprit who stabbed that housewife to death in east London, all those years ago? It all comes down to keeping an open mind on the matter.

There was one last matter that I wanted to try to resolve.

In June 2015, I drove to the east of England. I looked up at the large, detached house and remembered that fifty years previously, the nudes' murders enquiry was just coming to an end. Exactly four days previously, half a century ago, the decoy patrols had stood down and within another couple of weeks, the night patrols would finish.

I surveyed my surroundings. The house looked like an estate agent's dream; the striped lawn looked as though it had been manicured with nail scissors, the driveway was immaculate and on it stood a car, glistening with polish. I rang the doorbell and heard a dog bark; as the front door opened it ran out, wagging its tail in friendship. A 78-year-old man stood in the doorway, a lady behind him. In keeping with his extremely smart house, the man was dressed immaculately; but his eyes were so wild, he looked dishevelled.

I had found the Cop.

I asked him to confirm his identity and he did so. I said, 'My name is Dick Kirby and, like you, I was once a detective in the Metropolitan Police. Can I have a word with you?'

There was so much I wanted to ask him: and not in an accusatorial way, either. For instance, what direction had his life taken, post-prison? Was he aware that his name had been mentioned in several books about the Stripper, as well as a number of posts on the internet; and if he had, what was his reaction – anger? Contempt? Indifference? Whatever his emotions, did he wish to place on record – in this book – his feelings regarding the matter? Because if that was the case, I should be only too happy to accommodate him. However, I didn't get that far.

His jaw dropped before he recovered quickly. 'No, you can't!' he snapped. 'Bloody cheek you've got, coming round here!'

And that was that. The door was firmly shut and I walked back to my car. Why the hostile reception? He had no idea I was going to arrive, no idea what I wanted. Had I caught him at a bad moment? Whatever his reasoning, he'd made it clear that he didn't want to talk to me and, that being so, I certainly wasn't going to pester him; that was never my intention.

But as I started the drive to the North-west, and home, there was a thought nagging at my mind. I'd had only the briefest of glimpses at the Cop, just lasting seconds, but in that short space of time, I did think that he bore a similarity to the identikit picture that had received such a wide press circulation when it had been assembled half a century before.

If only he'd agreed to an hour's non-confrontational chat in relaxed surroundings, perhaps a closer and more searching look at him would have made me change my mind.

Let's face it, I have been wrong before.

CONCLUSION

So that was the story of the investigation into what became known as the Jack the Stripper Murders.

It's a story that, I venture to suggest, will never be resolved. In the same way that the Jack the Ripper investigation spawned suspects (and still does), more than three-quarters of a century prior to Jack the Stripper's depredations, so it was in this case; twenty-six of them.

Some, as you will now be aware, were so fatuous that all it required was a phone call, a look at documentation to prove the suspect's innocence so that they could be dusted down, apologised to and sent on their way. Others required a far more detailed look into their backgrounds and others still could never be completely eliminated from the enquiry.

But suspicion is never enough; what was required in this, and in all criminal cases, was cast iron evidence. You will also be aware that not one shred of direct evidence exists to put the Cop, Jock, the dentist, the garage owner or anybody else at the murder scenes.

Remember Spielberg's splendid film, *Raiders of the Lost Ark*? In the final sequence, a man pushes a trolley upon which reposes a wooden packing case, which in turn contains the Ark of the Covenant, into a secret warehouse, filled with similar, mysterious looking packing cases, each containing their own secrets. I mention this because, notwithstanding Spielberg's skilfully worded plot, I can assure you, nowhere – either in the National Archives,

New Scotland Yard or anywhere else – is there a secret file that contains the true identity of Jack the Stripper nor the proof as to his guilt.

But, as I say … if you're ever involved in a house clearance and you encounter a musty smelling trunk containing women's clothing and a tin that rattles – do let me know.

BIBLIOGRAPHY

Beveridge, Peter, *Inside the CID* (Evan Brothers Ltd, 1957).

Bowen, David, *Body of Evidence* (Constable, 2003).

Bunker, John, *From Rattle to Radio* (KAF Brewin Books, 1988).

Canter, David, *Criminal Shadows* (HarperCollins Publishers, 1994).

Capstick, John; with Thomas, Jack, *Given in Evidence* (John Long, 1960).

Cooper, Henry; with Giller, Norman *Henry Cooper's Most Memorable Fights* (Stanley Paul & Co. Ltd, 1985).

Cox, Barry; Shirley, John and Short, Martin, *The Fall of Scotland Yard* (Penguin Books, 1977).

Denning, Lord, *Lord Denning's Report* (Cmnd. 2152, HMSO, 1963).

Du Rose, John, *Murder was my Business* (W.H. Allen & Co., 1971).

Evans, Jimmy; Short, Martin, *The Survivor* (Mainstream Publishing, 2001).

Fido, Martin; Skinner, Keith, *The Official Encyclopedia of Scotland Yard* (Virgin Books, 1999).

Flynn, Errol, *My Wicked, Wicked Ways* (Pan Books Ltd, 1961).

Greeno, Edward, *War on the Underworld* (John Long, 1960).

Hart, Edward T, *Britain's Godfather* (True Crime Library, 1993).

Hatherill, George, *A Detective's Story* (Andre Deutsch Ltd, 1971).

Jackson, Sir Richard, *Occupied with Crime* (George G. Harrap & Co., 1967).

Kennedy, Ludovic, *The Trial of Stephen Ward* (Victor Gollancz Ltd, 1964).

Kirby, Dick, *Villains* (Robinson, 2008).

Kirby, Dick, *The Guv'nors – Ten of Scotland Yard's Greatest Detectives* (Wharncliffe True Crime, 2010).

Kirby, Dick, *The Sweeney – The First Sixty Years of Scotland Yard's Crimebusting Flying Squad 1919–1978* (Wharncliffe True Crime, 2011).

Kirby, Dick, *Scotland Yard's Ghost Squad – The Secret Weapon Against Post-war Crime* (Wharncliffe True Crime, 2011).

Kirby, Dick, *The Scourge of Soho – The Controversial Career of SAS Hero Detective Sergeant Harry Challenor, MM* (Pen & Sword True Crime, 2013).

Kirby, Dick, *Whitechapel's Sherlock Holmes* (Pen & Sword True Crime, 2014).

Knightley, Phillip; Kennedy, Caroline, *An Affair of State* (Jonathan Cape Ltd, 1987).

Lucas, Norman, *Britain's Gangland* (Pan Books Ltd, 1969).

McConnell, Brian, *Found Naked and Dead* (New English Library, 1974).

McKnight, Gerald, *The Murder Squad* (W. H. Allen & Co., 1967).

Mason, Fergus, *Exposing Jack the Stripper* (Absolute Crime Books, 2013).

Milkins, Neil, *Who was Jack the Stripper?* (Rose Heywood Press, 2011).

Mortimer, John, *Character Parts* (Viking Books, 1986).

Moss, Stirling, with Purdy, Ken W, *All But My Life* (William Kimber & Co. Ltd, 1963).

Payn, Graham; Morley, Sheridan, (Ed.) *The Noël Coward Diaries* (Weidenfeld & Nicolson, 1982).

Read, Leonard, with Morton, James, *Nipper* (Macdonald & Co. Ltd, 1991).

Seabrook, David, *Jack of Jumps* (Granta Books, 2006).

Thomas, Donald, *Villains' Paradise* (John Murray Publishers, 2005).

Wolfenden, Lord, *The Report of the Committee on Homosexual Offences and Prostitution* (Cmnd. 367, HMSO, 1957).

Woodland, David, *Crime and Corruption at the Yard* (Pen & Sword True Crime, 2015).

INDEX

The History Press

The destination for history
www.thehistorypress.co.uk